ANGLAIS APPLIQUÉ

Économie, Gestion,

Droit, AES

1er cycle

ANGLAIS APPLIQUÉ

Économie, Gestion,
Droit, AES
1er cycle

LESLIE THOMPSON

Maître de conférences à l'Université de Paris I
(Panthéon-Sorbonne)

JEAN-TOUSSAINT PINDI

Maître de conférences à l'Université de Paris I
(Panthéon-Sorbonne)

2e édition

Montchrestien

LANGUES APPLIQUÉES

Collection dirigée par L. THOMPSON
Maître de conférences à l'Université Paris 1 (Panthéon-Sorbonne)

Déjà parus :

L. THOMPSON et J.-T. PINDI, **Anglais appliqué : Gestion, Économie d'entreprise, Travail, Ressources Humaines,** 2e et 3e cycles, 2001, 206 pages

I. NOBLE, **Anglais appliqué : Droit, Science Politique**, 1er et 2e cycles, 2002, 210 pages

P. ARQUIMBAU-AMBLAT et J. MARTINEZ-DORRONSORO,
Espagnol appliqué : Économie, Gestion, Droit, AES, 1er et 2e cycles, 2002, 234 pages

31 rue Falguière, 75741 Paris Cedex 15
ISBN : 2-7076-1352-5

Dedicated to the memory of

OLIVIER STURGE-MOORE

CONTENTS

INTRODUCTION

Cette deuxième édition de l'ouvrage ***Anglais appliqué 1*** est destinée aux étudiants du premier cycle universitaire, désormais organisé en un cursus de trois années d'études aboutissant à la *Licence*, qui suivent un enseignement d'anglais dans le cadre de leurs études de Sciences économiques, de Gestion, de Droit ou d'AES. L'ouvrage peut également être utilisé pour enseigner l'anglais de spécialité dans les écoles de commerce, dans la filière Langues Etrangères Appliquées (LEA), dans certaines sections d'IUT et de BTS, et dans le cadre de la formation continue.

Il constitue pour le professeur d'anglais un support pédagogique visant à structurer les travaux dirigés d'anglais. Les six parties du livre abordent un ensemble de thèmes distincts relevant du monde économique ou juridique. La partie *Sociologie* qui figurait dans la première édition a été supprimée et remplacée par une partie *Management* par souci d'une plus grande complémentarité avec les sujets à caractère économique, axe disciplinaire majeur de l'ouvrage.

Il offre ainsi un vaste panorama de thèmes allant de l'économie féodale aux technologies de l'information et de la communication, en passant par la pensée de Smith, Ricardo, Malthus et Marx, la bourse, le protectionnisme, le syndicalisme et le marché du travail; des origines du droit à la profession d'avocat sans oublier l'organisation de l'entreprise moderne, le marketing, les fusions et acquisitions d'entreprises en Europe. Tous les articles d'actualité ont été renouvelés.

Nous considérons que nous nous devons d'encourager les étudiants à acquérir progressivement le plus d'autonomie possible dans la lecture de textes et d'articles traitant de différents sujets auxquels ils seront confrontés au cours de leurs études et dans leur vie professionnelle. Les documents choisis sont ainsi caractéristiques de différents *genres* et nous avons essayé d'en didactiser le discours spécialisé. De nombreux textes proviennent de manuels universitaires d'économie, de gestion et de droit, d'autres sont des articles d'actualité économique et juridique puisés dans différents quotidiens et hebdomadaires anglo-américains. Un article tiré d'une revue de recherches en sciences économiques complète le corpus. Nous espérons que l'ensemble des contenus, s'articulant avec des exercices variés, encouragera l'étudiant à mobiliser ses compétences linguistiques au service de l'esprit critique.

L'ouvrage comporte une soixantaine de nouveaux exercices. Chaque chapitre est, en règle générale, construit autour d'un ou de deux textes théoriques et d'un article d'actualité, complété d'exercices de compréhension, de vocabulaire et de grammaire. Le vocabulaire non technique et de spécialité imprimé en caractères gras est mis en exergue dans chaque chapitre sur une liste de *Key words and concepts*. Des termes spécialisés définis dans leur contexte sont placés immédiatement après le texte étudié et constituent un glossaire, *List of Definitions*, dont l'objet est d'aider l'étudiant à acquérir des bases lexicales spécialisées devant lui faciliter la compréhension du texte. Ces mêmes termes sont également exploités de façon plus active dans des exercices de vocabulaire. Cette disposition permet aux enseignants, comme aux étudiants, d'avoir un aperçu du vocabulaire enseigné dans le chapitre et de s'en servir pour des activités de pré- et de post-lecture. L'usage du dictionnaire unilingue n'en est pas moins conseillé. Le *Vocabulary aid*, qui figure dans certains chapitres, sert à régler rapidement le sens de quelques mots précis peu usuels. Dans tous les cas, l'étudiant est invité à se reporter à la rubrique *Instructions For Study* pour mener à bien l'étude de chaque chapitre. Des exercices de recherche sur *internet* ou des sujets de *Discussion* suggérés dans l'ouvrage visent à développer, à travers le support écrit, une synergie de toutes les compétences linguistiques des apprenants. Les exercices de compréhension permettent une lecture globale et approfondie du texte alors que les exercices de grammaire ont pour objectif d'aider l'étudiant à former des phrases correctes à l'écrit comme à l'oral, tout en restant dans un contexte disciplinaire précis. Ils ne sont pas accompagnés d'explications grammaticales et ne font pas l'objet d'une progression structurée. Tel n'est pas le propos de ce livre. Les *Glossary Exercises* permettent une révision générale des termes et concepts présentés dans chaque partie. Un répertoire de termes de spécialité exploités dans l'ouvrage se situe dans l'*Index* avec référence aux chapitres dans lesquels ils ont été abordés.

L'apport personnel de chaque enseignant reste, bien entendu, indispensable tout comme l'utilisation d'autres ressources pédagogiques permettant d'approfondir le contenu de ce livre. Aussi serions-nous très heureux de recevoir les avis et observations de nos collègues, anglicistes de spécialité, ou spécialistes des disciplines d'application, afin d'enrichir cet ouvrage et d'apporter les réponses les mieux adaptées aux attentes et aux besoins des étudiants. Ils peuvent être adressés à l'attention des auteurs :

Leslie.Thompson@univ-paris1.fr

Jean.Pindi@univ-paris1.fr

Leslie THOMPSON
et Jean-Toussaint PINDI

Un corrigé destiné aux professeurs est disponible auprès des auteurs sur justificatif de leur qualité d'enseignant

PART A

ECONOMIC HISTORY

IN THIS PART YOU WILL READ ABOUT

- The workings of a feudal economy and the rationale for the social system
- The beliefs of the Physiocrats and Quesnay's *Tableau Economique*
- The enclosure movement in sixteenth century England
- The Tudor poor laws and the Christian paternalist ethic
- Welfare and social democracy
- The profit-seeking motive and the transformation of rural England through the industrial revolution
- The knowledge economy

YOU WILL LEARN SOME BASIC ECONOMIC TERMS CONCERNING

- Farming and agriculture
- Social class
- Labour and crafts
- Manufacturing and mechanization
- Information technology

CHAPTER 1

THE FEUDAL ECONOMY

◇ Key words and concepts

rent
taxes
support
share
crop
investment in seed
yield
output
commodities
production
consumption
input-output table
landlords
peasants
artisans
stock
carry-over
harvest
surplus
manufactures
gross income
raw materials
value
wear and tear
deplete
ratio of surplus to stock
net product
wealth
landowner

◇ Vocabulary aid

seed	semence
loom	métier à tisser
weaver	tisserand
blacksmith	forgeron

Instructions For Study

1° Turn to the **definitions** following the text *The Feudal Economy*. They refer to the specialist terms printed in **bold** type in the list of **Key words and concepts.** Study them closely and pinpoint them in the text.
2° Use an **English** language dictionary to check the meanings (in context) of the other words in the list.
3° Do the exercises to test your comprehension, vocabulary and grammar skills.

The Feudal Economy

France in the eighteenth century maintained the structure of a feudal economy. The rent of land, along with taxes levied from the cultivators, was the source of funds to support the court, the army, and all the arts of civilization. Rent was simply taken from the peasants as a share of the crop. The peasants had to provide their own subsistence and the necessary investment in seed and so forth, out of the rest. The Physiocrats based their doctrines on this picture; in their view the land, which yields rent, is the only source of net output.

François Quesnay (1694-1774), who was a physician at the court of Louis XIV, is sometimes acclaimed as the first modern economist, for he set out his analysis of the economic system in terms of an abstract scheme illustrating the flows of commodities in the process of production and consumption. This table, which Quesnay based on the circulation of the blood, somewhat resembles an input-output table such as is nowadays used to show the structure of industrial production. There are three social classes: landlords, peasants, and artisans. If we simplify Quesnay's *Tableau Economique* somewhat, the relations between them are as follows.

At the beginning of each year, the peasants own a stock, the carry-over from last year's harvest. This feeds them and provides them with inputs of seed, etc., for a year; they cultivate the land and produce a crop which, in Quesnay's example, is twice the stock that they had to start with. With this, they replace the stock which has been consumed in the process or production; the surplus, or net output, they pay to the landlords. The landlords consume part directly–feeding their entourage–and the rest they use to buy the products of the artisans. The artisans own their productive equipment–a loom for the weaver, a forge for the blackmith. The payments that they receive for their manufactures are their gross income, out of which they both replace raw materials and wear and tear of equipment, and feed themselves. What they receive is just the value of their output. They do not contribute to the surplus. The only surplus comes from land.

These views supported certain progressive prescriptions for policy. Firstly, it was wrong to tax the peasants, for this would deplete the stock which is necessary for them to consume in the course of reproducing the surplus. Secondly, it was desirable to improve methods of cultivation to increase the ratio of surplus to stock and raise the net product, thus increasing the demand for the output of the artisans and the wealth of the nation in general. These were deductions from analysis concerned with the mechanism of the economy. But there was also a metaphysical side to the argument. Identifying surplus with the landlords' rent could be turned into a justification for the social system. Since only land produced a surplus, only the landowner had a right to enjoy it.

Joan Robinson & John Eatwell, *An Introduction to Modern Economics*, London: Mc Graw-Hill, 1973 (pp.8-9)

◇◇ DEFINITIONS ◇◇◇

- ♦**rent** a sum paid to the landlord for the use of land
- ♦**taxes** payments made to the legal authorities to meet public expenses
- ♦**crop** a plant cultivated in large quantities on farms and in fields (e.g.corn, rice); the plants collected at harvest time
- ♦**yield** to produce or to return an amount of food, plants or money (often expressed as a percentage)
- ♦**output** the goods produced (crops) using **inputs** (land, seed, labour)
- ♦**commodities** primary products such as wheat, wool or coffee; *economic goods*
- ♦**landlords** owners of land who rent it to others
- ♦**stock** the goods held (crops) for current and future consumption
- ♦**harvest** the crops picked or cut when ripe
- ♦**surplus** an amount left over after fulfilling immediate needs
- ♦**manufactures** the products made by the artisans
- ♦**gross income** total revenue from sales before any expenditure on raw materials or equipment
- ♦**raw materials** something used in manufacturing and transformed to make a finished product
- ♦**value** the worth of a good; what something is worth
- ♦**wear and tear** normal damage to equipment due to use
- ♦**wealth** the value of what is owned by someone; *riches*

◇◇ EXERCISES ◇◇◇

◇ EXERCISE 1 *Comprehension*

True / False Circle the correct choice and justify your answer

1. In eighteenth century France, the peasants paid rent in cash. T / F
2. The Physiocrats believed the land was the sole provider of net output. T / F
3. In Quesnay's example the surplus is equated with the net output. T / F
4. The peasants had to pay the landlords for their seed. T / F
5. The artisans earned their living by using their own tools. T / F
6. The Physiocrats encouraged economic growth. T / F

◇ EXERCISE 2 *Vocabulary*

(A) Select the verbs in the left hand column which **match** the nouns in the right-hand one

1. to levy	a) their own subsistence
2. to produce	b) stock
3. to provide	c) payments
4. to yield	d) the ratio
5. to own	e) taxes

6. to produce f) a crop
7. to receive g) a surplus
8. to deplete h) rent
9. to improve i) the stock
10. to increase j) methods

(B) **Fill in the blanks** with the words listed below

macroeconomic / surplus value / taxes / savings / yielded / a single tax / underconsumption / net income / flows / transactions

Quesnay's *Tableau Economique*

The *tableau* set out three classes of society, and showed how ....(1) flowed between them. The three classes were landowners, farmers and farm-labourers and others, called the 'sterile class'. Only the agricultural sector produced any ....(2) the rest only reproducing what it consumed. He anticipated Malthus's fear of ....(3) arising from excessive ....(4) Net income would be reduced if the ....(5) in the *tableau* were interrupted by delays in spending. This was the first attempt to construct a ....(6) input-output model of the economy. Quesnay suggested ....(7), *l'impôt unique*, on the ....(8) arguing that by so doing the nation would save tax-collecting costs. Only agriculture ....(9) a surplus, and therefore it bears all ....(10) ultimately anyway. He was the central figure in the group of economists called the Physiocrats, who flourished in France between 1760 and 1770.

◇ EXERCISE 3 *Grammar*

(A) Determiners
Supply the **missing articles** where necessary

The Physiocrats

A group of eighteenth-century French economists, led by F. Quesnay, who later became known as ....(1) *Physiocrats* or *Les Economistes*. They believed in ....(2) existence of ....(3) natural order and regarded ....(4) state's role as simply that of preserving ....(5) property and upholding ....(6) natural order. They held that ....(7) agriculture was ....(8) only source of wealth and therefore this sector should be taxed by *l'impôt unique*. In this, and in their advocacy for ....(9) free trade, their views were directly opposed to those of ....(10) mercantilists. In their belief in *laissez-faire*, they had much in common with, and certainly influenced, ...(11) classical economics, and especially Adam Smith. Quesnay's *Tableau économique*, published in 1758, has in it the origins of ....(12) modern ideas on ....(13) circulation of wealth and ....(14) nature of interrelationships in ....(15) economy.

(B) The Past
Put the *third* paragraph of *The Feudal Society* in the **simple past tense**.

CHAPTER 2

THE ENCLOSURE MOVEMENT

◇ Key words and concepts

watershed
sale
labor power
increase
nobility
formerly
grazing
booming
amount
labor
peak
tenants
support
feudal ties
labor force
consumers
working class
yeomen
bankrupted
debts
guilds
craftsmen
monopolize
secure
starvation

◇ Vocabulary aid

to usher in	annoncer
to strip of	priver de
to fence off	clôturer
to herd	rassembler

Instructions For Study

1° Turn to the **definitions** following the text *The Enclosure Movement*. They refer to the specialist terms printed in **bold** type in the list of **Key words and concepts.** Study them closely and pinpoint them in the text.
2° Use an **English** language dictionary to check the meanings (in context) of the other words in the list.
3° Do the exercises to test your comprehension, vocabulary and grammar skills.

The Enclosure Movement

The early sixteenth century is a watershed in European history. It marks the vague dividing line between the old, decaying feudal order and the rising capitalist system. After 1550, important social and economic changes began to occur with increasing frequency, each reinforcing the other and together ushering in the system of capitalism. Among the most important of these changes were those creating a working class that was systematically stripped of any control over the production process and forced into a situation in which the sale of its labor power was its only means of survival. The population of western Europe, which had been relatively stagnant for a century and a half, increased by nearly one-third in the sixteenth century and stood at about 70 million in 1600.

The increase in population was accompanied by the enclosure movement, which had begun in England as early as the thirteenth century. The feudal nobility, in ever-increasing need of cash, fenced off or enclosed lands that had formerly been used for communal grazing, using the lands to graze sheep to satisfy the booming English wool and textile industries' demand for wool. The sheep brought good prices, and a minimal amount of labor was needed to herd them.

The enclosure movement reached its peak in the late fifteenth and sixteenth centuries, when in some areas as many as three-fourths to nine-tenths of the tenants were forced out of the countryside and into the cities to try to support themselves. Subsequent waves of enclosure continued until well into the nineteenth century. The enclosures and the increasing population further destroyed the remaining feudal ties, creating a large new labor force–a labor force without land, without any tools or instruments of production, and with only labor power to sell. This migration to the cities meant more labor for the capitalist industries, more men for the armies and navies, more men to colonize new lands, and more potential consumers, or buyers of products.

But the enclosures and the increase in population were by no means the sole source of the new working class. Innumerable peasants, yeomen, and minor nobility were bankrupted by exorbitant increases in monetary rents. Mounting debts that could not be repaid ruined countless others. In the cities and towns the guilds came to be more and more concerned with the income levels of their members. It was obvious to the craftsmen and merchants in the guilds that steps taken to minimize their number would serve to monopolize their crafts and to increase their incomes. Increasing numbers of urban producers came to be denied any means of independent production as the guilds became more exclusive. Thus a considerable portion of the new working class was created within the towns and cities.

E.K. Hunt and Howard Sherman,
Economics, Harper & Row International Edition, 1986 (pp.18-19)

◊◊ DEFINITIONS ◊◊◊

- **sale** the selling of something for money
- **labor power** the worker's ability or capacity to produce
- **labor** human element of the production process; *work*
- **tenants** people who pay rent to landlords for the use of land or property
- **labor force** adults in employment or looking for a job
- **consumers** buyers of products and services who use them to satisfy their needs
- **working class** that part of the population, especially of lower socio-economic status, which works to earn a living,
- **yeomen** small farmers who cultivates their land, belonging to the class of freeholders below the gentry and nobility
- **guilds** historically an association of tradesmen or artisans which controlled production of a particular commodity or service and regulated the admission of members
- **craftsmen** skilled workmen or artisans who use their hands to make things

◊◊ EXERCISES ◊◊◊

◊ EXERCISE 1 *Comprehension*

True / False Circle the correct choice and justify your answer

1. The birth of capitalism is closely linked with the creation of the working class. T / F
2. The means of production remained in the hands of the working class. T / F
3. The sale of labor power became the only means of survival of the working class. T / F
4. Farmers were dispossessed and forced to migrate to the cities. T / F
5. Guilds encouraged workers to join them. T / F

◊ EXERCISE 2 *Vocabulary*

Use the list of definitions above to **select the appropriate term** to fit each sentence

1. Many urban producers such as craftsmen gradually lost any means of independent production.
2. Migration to the cities created markets for capitalist industry and large numbers of .consumers
3. As feudal ties were gradually destroyed, a growing ..class.. emerged in the cities.
4. The enclosures forced tenants out of the countryside who could only survive by selling their ..labor....power
5. Guilds. took measures to restrict their membership.

◇ EXERCISE 3 *Grammar*

Tenses

Complete the following paragraph with a **correct form** of the verb in brackets

Many of the farmers and craftsmen who (to be) were...(1) thus uprooted and (to deny) .denied.(2) access to their former means of production (to become) became.(3) vagabonds and beggars. Even more (to attempt) attempted.(4) to secure a subsistence by (to squat) squatting.(5) on marginal, unused lands where they could (to grow). .grow....(6) crops for their own use. Harshly repressive laws (to pass) .passed..(7) against such farming and against (to be) .being...(8) an unemployed vagabond. Thus when force, fraud, and starvation were insufficient (to create) ....(9) the new working class, criminal statutes and government repression (to use) ....(10).

THE POOR LAWS

◇ Key words and concepts

unemployment chômage
widespread répandu
deserving méritants
beg mendier
fund fond
pauper pauvre
supported aidé
compulsory obligatoire
rate taux
vagrants vagabonds
provisions dispositions
raw materials matières premières

statutes statut
framework structure
relief aide
apprenticed apprentis
trade profession
mercantilism
discharging transmettre
welfare bien-être
sin pécher
acknowledged reconnaissaient
deficiencies insuffisances

◇ Vocabulary aid

tractable	accomodant
parish	paroisse, commune
to board out	mettre en pension
to be predicated upon	être fondé sur

Instructions For Study

1° Turn to the **definitions** following the text *The Poor Laws*. They refer to the specialist terms printed in **bold** type in the list of **Key words and concepts.** Study them closely and pinpoint them in the text.
2° Use an **English** language dictionary to check the meanings (in context) of the other words in the list.
3° Do the exercises to test your comprehension, vocabulary and grammar skills.

The Poor Laws

Poor laws passed in 1531 and 1536 attempted to deal with the problems of unemployment, poverty, and misery then widespread in England. The first sought to distinguish between "deserving" and "undeserving" poor. Only the deserving poor were allowed to beg. The second decreed that each individual parish throughout England was responsible for its poor and that the parish should, through voluntary contributions, maintain a poor fund. This proved completely inadequate, and the "pauper problem" grew increasingly severe.

Finally, in 1572 the state accepted the principle that the poor would have to be supported by tax funds and enacted a compulsory "poor rate". And in 1576 "houses of correction" for "incorrigible vagrants" were authorized and provisions made for the parish to purchase raw materials to be worked up by the more tractable paupers and vagrants. Between that time and the close of the sixteenth century, several other poor-law statutes were passed.

The Poor Law of 1601 was the Tudor attempt to integrate these laws into one consistent framework. Its main provisions included formal recognition of the right of the poor to receive relief, imposition of compulsory poor rates at the parish level, and provision for differential treatment for various classes of the poor. The aged and the sick could receive help in their homes; pauper children who were too young to be apprenticed in a trade were to be boarded out; the deserving poor and unemployed were to be given work as provided for in the act of 1576; and incorrigible vagrants were to be sent to houses of correction and prisons.

From the preceding discussion it is possible to conclude that the period of English mercantilism was characterized by acceptance, in the spirit of the Christian paternalist ethic, of the idea that "the state had an obligation to serve society by accepting and discharging the responsibility for the general welfare." The various statutes passed during this period "were predicated upon the idea that poverty, instead of being a personal sin, was a function of the economic

system." They acknowledged that those who were the victims of the deficiencies of the economic system should be cared for by those who benefited from the system.

E.K. Hunt and Howard Sherman,
Economics, Harper & Row International Edition, 1986 (pp.28-29)

◇◇ DEFINITIONS ◇◇◇

- **unemployment** the situation of being out of work when willing and able to work
- **fund** a reserve of money put aside for a specific purpose
- **rate** a tax levied according to a certain scale
- **raw materials** something used in manufacturing and transformed to make a finished product
- **statutes** laws passed by Parliament
- **relief** financial assistance to the needy
- **trade** a manual occupation requiring a high degree of skill (e.g. carpenter)
- **mercantilism** 17th century economic philosophy stressing trade and commerce as the source of a nation's wealth, encouraging exports and restricting imports so as to accumulate gold

◇◇ EXERCISES ◇◇◇

◇ EXERCISE 1 *Comprehension*

True / False Circle the correct choice and justify your answer

1. The Poor Laws set up different classes of poor T / F
2. The "undeserving poor" were not allowed to beg T / F
3. The "pauper problem" worsened because nothing was done about it T / F
4. Elderly people were given special consideration T / F
5. The "poor rate" was always paid on a voluntary basis T / F
6. Pauper children were given the opportunity to learn a trade T / F
7. All vagrants were sent to prison T / F
8. The Poor Laws were based on the belief that people only had themselves to blame for their own poverty T / F

◇ EXERCISE 2 *Vocabulary*

Fill in the blanks with the words listed below

provisions / workhouses / rise / depress / labour / dependent / support / distribution / support / shares

The Condition of the Poor

The poor laws tended to ....(1) the general condition of the poor in two ways. First of all, they increased the population without increasing its supply of food. A poor man could marry with little or no prospect of being able to ....(2) a family. Thus they may be said to have created the poor to some extent, and, because of the growing population, as the ....(3) of the country had to be distributed to every man in smaller proportions, it is evident that the ....(4) of those who did not receive parish assistance would purchase a smaller quantity of provisions than previously and more of them would be led to ask for ....(5). Secondly, the quantity of provisions consumed in ....(6) by a part of society that could not in general be considered as the most valuable one reduced the ....(7) that would otherwise have belonged to more industrious and more worthy members, and thus more were forced to become ....(8). If the poor in the workhouses lived better, this new ....(9) of money worsened the condition of those out of the workhouses by occasioning a .... (10) in the price of provisions.

Based on T. R. Malthus: *An Essay on the Principle of Population* (1789)

◇ EXERCISE 3 ***Grammar***

The Active Voice

With the help of the text, turn the following sentences into the **active voice**. Remember that you will need to add a new subject to your sentences.

1. Only the deserving poor were allowed to beg.
2. A compulsory "poor rate" was enacted.
3. In 1576 "houses of correction" for "incorrigible vagrants" were authorized.
4. Several poor laws were passed.
5. The unemployed were to be given work.

DEBATE

NEW LABOUR AND WELFARE

From welfare to workhouse for the poor

◇ EXERCISE

Read the article below and discuss or write answers to the following questions

1. What is the philosophy behind the idea that "relief from destitution should be the task of the state"?
2. What does *noblesse oblige* refer to here?
3. What are some of the unintended effects of employer control over the working day?
4. Comment on the statement "it seems that the rich get the rights and the poor get the responsibilities"
5. What is left of the social democratic idea?

From welfare to workhouse for the poor

On both sides of the Atlantic, politicians have in recent years started to make a lot of personal responsibility. In November, Tony Blair explained that "from the 1940s to the 1970s... social democrats in Britain and the US who held a liberal view of the 'permissive society' divorced fairness from personal responsibility. They believed that the state had an unconditional obligation to provide welfare and security".

Instead, the New Labour line is that the means of subsistence should be made contingent upon willingness to take any job, whatever the pay or conditions. This was preceded in the US by the end of "welfare as we know it", signed into law by President Bill Clinton, under the wonderful title of "The Work Opportunity and Personal Responsibility Reconciliation Act".

There is nothing new about the idea that rights carry responsibilities. Conservatives from Benjamin Disraeli to Harold Macmillan would have recognised it as *noblesse oblige:* the idea that, as the *Oxford English Dictionary* puts it, privilege entails responsibility. President John F. Kennedy said (following the parable in Luke 12:48) that "of those to whom much is given, much is required". Those who have benefited most from the existing system of rights – the rich and powerful – are those who bear the heaviest responsibilities, because the way in which they use their advantages largely determines the fate of the rest of society.

Social democracy – the butt of Mr Blair's scorn – arose out of the contention that the security of ordinary people should not depend on this kind of goodwill. Charles Dickens, as George Orwell observed, never achieved this viewpoint, even though "in every page of his work one can see a consciousness that society is wrong somewhere at the root". Even in *Hard Times,* "the whole moral is that capitalists should be kind, not that workers should be rebellious".

The social democratic idea, whose remaining accomplishments Mr Blair is busy dismantling, was that workers should not have to depend on the kindness of capitalists for protection from hazardous conditions, long hours and pay too low to enable a family to live decently. Strong trade unions backed by decisive state intervention – anathema to both Mr Blair and to Margaret Thatcher – should provide the countervailing power to that of capitalists. Similarly, relief from destitution should be the task of the state, not something left to the whims of the "superhumanly kind old gentleman".

New Labour is equally contemptuous of *noblesse oblige* and the social democratic critique. Mr Blair is silent on the huge pay rises received by company directors, even when their companies have done badly or indeed gone bankrupt. Moreover, his enthusiasm for the notion of "stakeholding" did not survive the realisation that it would entail diluting the rights of shareholders by adding to the boards of companies representatives of other interests.

So, far from putting people before profits, we find Mr Blair and his newfound soul mate Silvio Berlusconi, the rightwing Italian prime minister, preaching labour flexibility. Yet it is precisely this control over the working day by employers that contributes to the juvenile delinquency deplored by Mr Blair. A recent American study showed that after allowing for differences in family income, parental education, marital status and total hours worked, parents who had to work at night were still 2.7 times as likely to have a child suspended from school.

When he was shadow home secretary and still had to carry the Labour party with him, Mr Blair famously talked about being "tough on crime and tough on the causes of crime". But the notion that crime has causes (such as labour flexibility) does not sit well with the exaltation of personal responsibility, so it is hardly surprising that we have heard no more of it since he became prime minister.

If the government's other priorities are school achievement and health, flexibility is again an impediment: holding all the same factors constant, the children of parents who worked nights scored only about two-thirds of the marks of others on tests for mathematical and reading abilities. As far as health is concerned, according to Harvard's Jody Heymann (Boston Review, February/March 2002), "when their parents are present, sick children... recover more quickly from illnesses and injuries. Furthermore, the presence of parents shortens children's hospital stays by 31 per cent".

Why do people accept jobs that have such manifestly deleterious consequences for their children's behaviour, education and health? Because the doctrine of rights and responsibilities does not permit them to insist on taking only jobs compatible with their responsibilities to their children, without losing income support.*

In the end, it turns out that the rights of property owners and employers are not to depend on their responsible use of them. There is only one group whose rights are to be conditional on good behaviour, as defined by the government, and that is recipients of means-tested welfare benefits. Rights and responsibilities, indeed – but it seems that the rich get the rights and the poor get the responsibilites.

Brian Barry, *Financial Times*,
2 January 2003 (p.9)

The writer is professor of political philosophy at Columbia University

* **income support** a non-contributory benefit paid by the government to people in great financial need, such as unemployed workers who are no longer eligible for unemployment benefit, one-parent families and the elderly.

CHAPTER 3

THE INDUSTRIAL REVOLUTION

◇ Key words and concepts

foreign étranger
goods biens
domestic intérieur
output production
export exportation
figures chiffres
profits profits
accounted for expliquer
eventually finalement
ban interdire
outlined souligner
cottage industry ind. artisanale
drive effort
inconsequential inconséquent
depleted épuisé
import importation
widespread répandue
work force main d'œuvre
mining exploitation minière

◇ Vocabulary aid

calico	calicot
to spur	accélérer
iron	fer
charcoal	charbon de bois
smelting	la fonte
pig iron	saumon de fonte
steam engine	machine à vapeur
to vault	franchir d'un saut

Instructions For Study

1° Turn to the **definitions** following the text *The Industrial Revolution*. They refer to the specialist terms printed in **bold** type in the list of **Key words and concepts.** Study them closely and pinpoint them in the text.
2° Use an **English** language dictionary to check the meanings (in context) of the other words in the list.
3° Do the exercises to test your comprehension, vocabulary and grammar skills.

The Industrial Revolution

Between 1700 and 1770 the foreign markets for English goods grew much faster than did England's domestic markets. During the period 1700-1750, output of domestic industries increased by 7 percent, while that of export industries increased by 76 percent. For the period of 1750-1770, the figures are 7 percent and 80 percent, respectively. This rapidly increasing foreign demand for English manufactures was the single most important cause of the most fundamental transformation of human life in history: the Industrial Revolution.

In this England, larger outputs of manufactured goods produced at lower prices meant ever-increasing profits. Thus profit seeking was the motive that, stimulated by increasing foreign demand, accounted for the virtual explosion of technological innovations that occurred in the late eighteenth and early nineteenth centuries, radically transforming all England and eventually most of the world.

The textile industry was the most important in the early Industrial Revolution. In 1700 the woolen industry had persuaded the government to ban the import of Indian-made "calicoes" (cotton) and thus had secured a protected home market for domestic producers. As outlined earlier, rising foreign demand spurred mechanization of the industry. Textile manufacturing in England was rapidly transformed from a cottage to a factory industry.

The iron industry was also very important in the early drive to mechanized factory production. In the early eighteenth century England's iron industry was quite inconsequential. Charcoal was still used for smelting, as it had been since prehistoric times. By this time, however, the forests surrounding the iron mines were almost completely depleted. England was forced to import pig iron from its colonies, as well as from Sweden, Germany, and Spain. In 1709, Abraham Darby developed a process for making coke from coal for use in the smelting process.

Despite the relative abundance of coal near the iron mines, it was not until the latter part of the eighteenth century (when military demands on the arms and munitions industries were very great) that the iron industry began using coke extensively. A whole series of innovations followed, leading to a very rapid expansion of the iron and coal-mining industries, which permitted the increasingly widespread use of machines made of iron in a great variety of industries.

Entrepreneurs in many other industries saw the possibilites for larger profits if they could increase output and lower costs. In this period there was a veritable outburst of inventive activity.

Undoubtedly the most important of these innovations was the development of the steam engine. Industrial steam engines had been introduced in the early 1700s, but mechanical difficulties had limited their use to the pumping of water in mines.

By the turn of the next century steam was rapidly replacing water as the chief source of power in manufacturing. The development of steam power led to profound economic and social changes.

The growth in the major manufacturing cities was truly spectacular. For example, the population of Manchester rose from 17,000 in 1760 to 237,000 in 1831 and 400,000 in 1851. Output of manufactured goods approximately doubled in the second half of the eighteenth century and grew even more rapidly in the early nineteenth century. By 1801 nearly 30 percent of the English work force was employed in manufacturing and mining; by 1831 this figure had risen to more than 40 percent. Thus the Industrial Revolution transformed England into a country of large urban manufacturing centers, where the factory system was dominant. The result was a very rapid growth of productivity that vaulted England into the position of the greatest economic and political power of the nineteenth century.

E.K. Hunt and Howard Sherman,
Economics, Harper & Row International Edition, 1986 (pp.35-38)

◇◇ DEFINITIONS ◇◇◇

- **goods** products; objects which have undergone transformation during the process of production
- **output** the goods produced (textiles) using inputs (cotton)
- **export** shipping goods from one country to another for sale or exchange
- **profits** the income accruing to the entrepreneur; *earnings*
- **cottage industry** production activity in which the work is done in the producer's own home
- **import** bringing goods in from foreign countries
- **work force** adults in employment or looking for a job; *labor force*

◇◇ EXERCISES ◇◇◇

◇ EXERCISE 1 *Comprehension*

True / False Circle the correct choice and justify your answer

1. The growth of home markets outpaced that of export markets in 18th century England. T / F
2. Increasing profits resulted from a decrease in production costs. T / F
3. New technology transformed most of the world. T / F
4. England had to import pig iron because it wanted to preserve its forests. T / F
5. Machines were used increasingly thanks to the growth of mining. T / F
6. Steam engines were used extensively in the early 1700s. T / F
7. Between 1801 and 1831 the industrial labor force rose only very gradually. T / F
8. The factory system was the principal factor behind rapid growth in productivity. T / F

◇ EXERCISE 2 *Vocabulary*

Fill in the blanks with the words listed below

The Use of Steam

resources / suitable / geographical / erected / stage / growth / price / enabled / century / network

The invention of the steam engine ushered in the final and most decisive ....(1) of the Industrial Revolution. The use of steam was not, like that of water, dependent on ....(2) position and local ....(3). Whenever coal could be brought at a reasonable ....(4) a steam engine could be ....(5). England had plenty of coal, and by the end of the eighteenth ....(6) it was already applied to many different uses, while a ....(7) of waterways, made on purpose, ...(8) it to be carried everywhere cheaply; the whole country became a privileged land, ...(9) above all others for the ....(10) of industry.

◇ EXERCISE 3 *Grammar*

The Passive Voice

Rewrite these sentences in the **passive voice**

Example: Increasing foreign demand stimulated profit seeking.
Profit seeking was stimulated by increasing foreign demand.

1. The Industrial Revolution radically transformed England and eventually the rest of the world.
2. The woollen industry had persuaded the government to ban the import of Indian cotton.
3. Abraham Darby developed a process for making coke from coal.
4. The iron industry began using coke extensively.
5. By the turn of the century steam was rapidly replacing water as the chief source of power in manufacturing.

ECONOMIC SCENE

INFORMATION TECHNOLOGY

The Industrial Revolution's 'Internet'

◇ EXERCISE

Read the article below and discuss or write answers to the following questions

1. What is the main advantage of the "knowledge economy"?
2. What changed in the 19th century?
3. Is Diderot's *Encyclopédie* a "search engine"?
4. What did medieval inventors lack?
5. What is meant by "the end of pure science"?

The Industrial Revolution's 'Internet'

NEW YORK: The "knowledge economy" did not begin or end with the Internet boom. But technology, institutions and attitudes that lower the cost of information and encourage people to share knowledge have not always been around.

Indeed, a new book argues, to understand why the West not only grew rich after the Industrial Revolution but kept growing richer, we have to understand the revolution in how people organize and exchange "useful knowledge."

"The main thing I'm interested in is how societies can end up knowing more and how that changes us," said Joel Mokyr, an economic historian at Northwestern University and author of "The Gifts of Athena" (Princeton University Press).

Throughout most of human history, periods of invention did not create sustained economic growth. Population might increase because, say, agricultural yields improved. But eventually the standard of living returned to its old equilibrium.

That pattern changed in the 19th century. Individual inventions not only flourished but sparked still more inventions and continuing economic growth.

"The true question of the Industrial Revolution is not why it took place at all but why it was sustained beyond, say, 1820," Mokyr writes.

The reason, he argues, lies in what he calls the Industrial Enlightenment, a series of cultural changes that connected practical and theoretical knowledge and made both more widely accessible. Through "search engines" ranging from Diderot's massive Encyclopedie to handbooks and periodicals, "useful knowledge" traveled from individual practitioners to anyone with an interest in improving techniques.

"The idea that knowledge is power did not translate into the idea that knowledge should be monopolized," Mokyr said in an interview. Instead, the ideal of "open science" prevailed. Even patents required, in exchange for economic protection, that inventors make their ideas public.

In addition, the Industrial Enlightenment "sought to understand why techniques worked by generalizing them" – a critical step in turning new knowledge into an engine of ongoing progress.

"In the Middle Ages, they invented lots of things," Mokyr said. "But the people who invented things were people out in the field who were smart and came up with things" by trial and error.

These inventors had no connection to the educated elite, and they had no general theories to explain and extend their inventions. Medieval inventors could not generalize from a water mill to the laws of hydraulics, for instance. Without widely applicable scientific theories, one invention was not likely to lead to another;

"In 1796 Edward Jenner invents vaccination, but he has no clue why it works", Mokyr noted. "There is no other vaccination for almost another 100 years, because nobody has an idea why it works."

The third important aspect of the Industrial Enlightenment was the bridges it built between "those who controlled propositional knowledge", including scientific generalizations, "and those who carried out the techniques contained in prescriptive knowledge", the know-how of fields such as agriculture, engineering and navigation. Practitioners and theorists no longer remained socially or intellectually isolated from one another.

In a sense, the Industrial Enlightenment was the end of "pure science." Now, "knowledge isn't just because we're curious and we want to know things, but because we're going to do something with it," Mokyr said.

** Virginia Postrel is the author of "The Future and Its Enemies."*

PART B

ECONOMIC THOUGHT

IN THIS PART YOU WILL READ ABOUT

- The beliefs of Adam Smith, the founding father of economics
- Malthus's principle of population
- Ricardo's labor theory of value
- Marx's theory of surplus value
- Keynes and the paradox of thrift
- Globalization

YOU WILL LEARN SOME BASIC ECONOMIC TERMS CONCERNING

- The division of labor
- Trade and commerce
- The process of production
- Saving and investment
- Fiscal policy

CHAPTER 4

ADAM SMITH

◇ Key words and concepts

trade
customs
official
bother
reap
reward
wealth
enhanced
division of labor
line of business
occupational
skill
assembly line
attendant
labor productivity
production runs
tariffs
goods

◇ Vocabulary aid

diligence	assiduité
sloth	paresse
predacious	rapace
pin	épingle
wire	fil de fer
to grind	meuler
scope	champ ou rayon d'action

Instructions For Study

1° Turn to the **definitions** following the text *Adam Smith*. They refer to the specialist terms printed in **bold** type in the list of **Key words and concepts.** Study them closely and pinpoint them in the text.
2° Use an **English** language dictionary to check the meanings (in context) of the other words in the list.
3° Do the exercises to test your comprehension, vocabulary and grammar skills.

Adam Smith

The greatest of Scotchmen was the first economist, Adam Smith. Economists do not have a great reputation for agreeing with one another – but on one thing there is wide agreement. If economics has a founding father, it is Smith. He was born, or anyhow baptized, in the small port town of Kirkcaldy on the north side of the Firth of Forth in 1723. The father of the man whose name would ever after be linked with freedom of trade was a customs official.

Smith went to the good local school and on to Oxford University. His impressions of Oxford were adverse; he later held that the Oxford public professors, as those with a salary were called, did no work. They got their pay anyway so why should they bother. The professors were a metaphor of his economic system.

Men – and women – do their best when they reap both the rewards of diligence or intelligence and the penalties of sloth. It was equally important that people be free to seek the work or conduct the business that would reward their efforts. What so served the individual, got him the most, then best served the society by getting it the most.

The wealth of a nation results from the diligent pursuit by each of its citizens of his own interests – when he reaps the resulting reward or suffers any resulting penalties. In serving his own interests, the individual serves the public interest. In Smith's greatest phrase, he is guided to do so as though by an unseen hand. Better the unseen hand than the visible, inept and predacious hand of the state.

Along with the pursuit of self-interest, the wealth of a nation was also enhanced by the division of labor. To this – broadly speaking, the superior efficiency of specialization – Smith attributed the greatest importance. Some of the gains in efficiency were from specialization by line of business and some from occupational specialization; some were from the fact that countries specialized in particular products or lines of trade. Some gains were from specialization within the industrial process. "The greatest improvement in the productive powers of labour, and the greater part of the skill, dexterity, and judgment with which it is anywhere directed, or applied, seem to have been the effects of the division of labour."

Here is how Smith described the division of labor in his most notable case; in his pursuit of information he must have encountered the manufacture of pins and observed the process with his usual care:

> One man draws out the wire, another straights it, a third cuts it, a fourth points it, a fifth grinds it at the top for receiving the head; to make the head requires two or three distinct operations; to put it on, is a peculiar business, to whiten the pins is another; it is even a trade by itself to put them into the paper...

Ten men so dividing the labor, Smith calculated, could make 48,000 pins a day, 4800 apiece. One man doing all the operations would make maybe one, maybe twenty. It is still widely believed that the assembly line, with its attendant increase in labor productivity, was the invention early in the present century of Henry Ford.

The larger the market, the longer could be the production runs – pins or whatever – and the greater the opportunity for the division of labor. From this came Smith's case against tariffs and other restraints on trade and for the greatest possible freedom, national and international, in the exchange of goods, the widest possible market.

Freedom of trade, in its turn, enlarged the freedom of the individual in the pursuit of his self-interest. His scope became not national but international. From the combination of freedom of trade and freedom of enterprise came a yet larger production of what was most wanted – the most favorable social result.

J.K. Galbraith, *The Age of Uncertainty*,
London: BBC & A. Deutsch, 1977 (pp.13, 15, 22-23)

◇◇ DEFINITIONS ◇◇◇

- ♦**trade** the activity of exchanging, or buying and selling goods; commerce
- ♦**customs** government department which controls the import and export of goods and collects import duties (taxes)
- ♦**wealth** the value of what is owned; *riches*
- ♦**division of labor** a form of production in which each worker or group of workers specializes in a single job or limited number of work tasks
- ♦**skill** the ability to use one's knowledge or proficiency to perform a task
- ♦**assembly line** a system of mass production in which units being assembled move slowly along a line of workers each of whom performs a given operation
- ♦**labor productivity** the quantity of articles produced per worker per unit of time
- ♦**tariffs** customs duties (taxes) levied (raised) by a government on imported or exported goods
- ♦**goods** products; objects which have undergone transformation during the process of production

◇◇ EXERCISES ◇◇◇

◇ EXERCISE 1 — *Comprehension*

True / False Circle the correct choice and justify your answer

1. Smith's name is linked with freedom of trade. T / F
2. What serves the individual also serves public interest. T / F
3. The visible hand of the State is necessary to control the economy. T / F
4. The concept underlying the assembly line was developed by Henry Ford. T / F
5. The division of labour revolutionized working conditions. T / F
6. Smith favoured imposing tariffs and controlling import and export activities. T / F

◇ EXERCISE 2 — *Vocabulary*

Use the list of definitions above to **select the appropriate term** to fit each sentence

1. Smith believed that the enemy of freedom of trade was the interventionist government that imposed ....
2. The invention of the steam engine greatly increased .... in the textile industry.
3. Production and trade, far less hampered than in other countries, brought the British nation all the .... that Adam Smith had promised.
4. The classical liberals were firm believers in the economic benefits of the ....
5. The market would lead to a constant striving to improve the quality of .... and to organize production in the most efficient and least costly manner.

◇ EXERCISE 3 *Grammar*

Tenses

Complete the following paragraph with the correct form of the verb in brackets

Smith (*to be*) (1) primarily concerned with the factors which (*to lead*) (2) to increased wealth in a community, and he (*to reject*) (3) the physiocrats' view of the pre-eminent position of agriculture, (*to recognize*) (4) the parallel contribution of manufacturing industry. He (*to begin*) (5) his analysis by means of a sketch of a primitive society of hunters. If it (*to cost*) (6) twice the labour (*to kill*) (7) a beaver as it (*to do*) (8) a deer, one beaver (*to exchange*) (9) for two deer. Labour (*to be*) (10) the fundamental measure of value, though actual prices of commodities (*to be*) (11) determined by supply and demand.

RICARDO AND MALTHUS

◇ Key words and concepts

competition
prices
rough
rearing
sustaining
labor
shape
labor theory of value
mankind
contender
stockbroker
clergyman
damaging
supply
likely
checks
rewards
trade
division of labor
bare
fate
wages
wasted
trade unions
landlord
rents
accruing to
investment
provided
income
shortage
purchasing power
depressions
offset

◇ Vocabulary aid

ghastly	épouvantable
dismal	triste
pregnant	d'une grande portée
to shove up	augmenter
to demur	objecter
to falter	vaciller
crackpot	cinglé

Instructions For Study

1° Turn to the **definitions** following the text *Ricardo and Malthus*. They refer to the specialist terms printed in **bold** type in the list of **Key words and concepts.** Study them closely and pinpoint them in the text.
2° Use an **English** language dictionary to check the meanings (in context) of the other words in the list.
3° Do the exercises to test your comprehension, vocabulary and grammar skills.

Ricardo and Malthus

Adam Smith offered more than counsel on public affairs. He offered what would today be called an economic model – a view of how the economic system works. Competition caused prices to be set in rough accord with the cost of production. The cost of production of an item, in turn, was the cost of reproducing, rearing and sustaining the labor that went into it.

Here were the germs of two ideas which were to grow and shape men's thought – and which still do. One was the labor theory of value. The other was that mankind would tend always to fall victim to its own fecundity: the never-to-be-repressed population explosion.

In the twenty-five years following Adam Smith's death, both ideas were taken up in London by two close friends, David Ricardo and Thomas Malthus. Ricardo is Smith's only serious contender for the title of founding father of economics; with him the great ethnic rivals of the Scotch arrive. Ricardo was Jewish. He was a stockbroker, a member of Parliament, a man of superb clarity of mind and terrible obscurity of prose. Malthus, a nonpracticing clergyman, was English.

From Malthus came the Principle of Population. This held that, given "the passion between the sexes" (a most damaging thing that he sometimes thought might be subject to "moral restraint" and against which he suggested ministers might warn at marriage), population would always increase in geometric ratio – 2, 4, 8, 16 and so on. Meanwhile, at best, the food supply would increase only arithmetically – 2, 3, 4, 5... From this came the inevitable result: in the likely absence of moral restraint, population would be subject only to the recurrent and ghastly checks imposed by famine or by war or natural catastrophe. Adam Smith, reflecting on the rewards from the freedom of trade, the resulting pursuit of self-interest and the division of labor, had a generally optimistic view of the prospects for man. Not Malthus. Nor was David Ricardo ever thought an optimist. It was with Malthus and Ricardo that economics became the dismal science.

Equally with his friend, David Ricardo foresaw a continuing increase in population, and Malthus's population became Ricardo's workers. Among the workers would be such competition for work on the one hand and for the food supply on the other that all would be reduced to bare subsistence. It was man's fate.

In an "improving society" this fate might be postponed, and, as a moment's thought will suggest, in the England of the nineteenth century this was a major qualification. But Ricardo's qualifications never caught up with his majestic generalizations. In the Ricardian world workers would receive the minimum necessary for life, never more. This was the iron law of wages. It led, among other things, to the conclusion that not only was compassion wasted on the working man but it was damaging. It might raise hopes and income in the short run. But it accelerated the population increase by which both were brought down. And any effort by government or trade unions to raise wages and rescue people from poverty would similarly be in conflict with economic law, be similarly frustrated by the resulting increase in numbers.

Different products of farms or factories required different amounts of Ricardo's minimally nourished labor. The amount of labor required established the relative value of things – again the labor theory of value. This, in turn, nurtured the distinctly pregnant thought that, since labor set the value of things, the whole product belonged to labor. Voiced in slightly different form by Marx half a century on, this proposal would shake the world.

Ricardo's world was still strongly rural. By the early decades of the nineteenth century, the Industrial Revolution was in the full thrust of change. However, in Ricardo's system the main figure was still the landlord. The same pressure of people on land that reduced wages had the effect of shoving up rents. In consequence, the more numerous the people, the richer were the landlords. They fattened, their people starved. And again nothing could be done about it; to return some of the rent to the farm workers would only cause their numbers to increase.

In Ricardo's world the state was receding in importance and power. It was the continuing lesson of Adam Smith that it should. Intervention by government would not, as noted, help the poor. But it would limit economic freedom and the pursuit of self-interest and thus make everything worse. David Ricardo was not, by his own lights, a cruel man. In a naturally cruel world he merely urged against contending in a futile way with the inevitable and for accepting the least bad. He did provide the rich with a very satisfactory formula for suffering the misfortunes of the poor.

There was a difference of opinion of much future importance between the two friends over what would happen to the handsome revenue accruing to the landlords. Ricardo held that it would either be spent or it would be saved and used for investment in land improvement, building, industrial development, in which case it would also be spent. He accepted a proposition made earlier by Jean Baptiste Say, the great French interpreter of Adam Smith. Say's Law held that production always provided the income to buy whatever was produced. What was saved was also spent, only in a different way, so there could never be a shortage of purchasing power.

On this point Malthus demurred. Perhaps the revenue might go unspent; perhaps there might, in consequence, be a shortage of purchasing power; perhaps, as a further consequence, the economy would, on occasion, falter and break down. There would be depressions resulting from a shortage of purchasing power as part of the natural order of things.

This too was a pregnant thought but it did not take. Ricardo's view, as Keynes was later to say, captured Britain as the Holy Inquisition captured Spain. For the next hundred years, until the decade of the Great Depression, Say and Ricardo ruled supreme. Men who said there could be a shortage of purchasing power did not know their economics; in fact, they were considered crackpots. Then, with John Maynard Keynes, Malthus's idea of a shortage of purchasing power became accepted doctrine. The most urgent task of government now was to compensate for the shortage, to offset the oversaving. Economics is not an exact science.

J.K. Galbraith, *The Age of Uncertainty*,
London, BBC & A. Deutsch, 1977 (pp.32, 35-36)

◇◇ DEFINITIONS ◇◇◇

- **competition** rivalry between different firms for the same customers
- **price** value expressed in terms of money
- **labor** human element of the production process; *work*
- **labor theory of value** the basis of value of an economic good is the amount of labor required to produce it
- **stockbroker** an agent who buys and sells stocks and shares on a stock exchange and who is paid a commission by his clients for this service
- **supply** the quantity of a good available on the market
- **trade** the activity of exchanging, or buying and selling of goods; *commerce*
- **division of labor** a form of production in which each worker or group of workers specializes in a single job or limited number of work tasks
- **wages** income for manual labor
- **trade unions** organizations of workers set up to protect and promote their rights and interests
- **landlords** owners of land who rent it to others
- **rents** sums paid to the landlord for the use of land
- **investment** expenditure on property aimed at returning an income
- **income** the money returned from the use of land, labor or capital; earnings
- **shortage** lack, scarcity or insufficient supply of something
- **purchasing power** the amount of goods and services you can actually buy with your money income
- **depression** a large and persistent fall in the level of output and employment

◇◇ EXERCISES ◇◇◇

◇ EXERCISE 1 *Comprehension*

True / False Circle the correct choice and justify your answer

1. Smith believed that the production cost of a good was equal to its selling price. T / F
2. Ricardo and Malthus rejected Smith's ideas. T / F
3. Malthus encouraged birth control. T / F
4. Malthus, Ricardo and Smith were *all* optimists. T / F
5. Both Ricardo and Malthus believed man was destined to live with no more than the basic necessities of life. T / F
6. Ricardo believed that some rent should be transferred to the farm workers. T / F

◇ EXERCISE 2 *Vocabulary*

(A) Find words or expressions in the text with equivalent terms to those in italics below

1. Ricardo and Malthus *worked on* two ideas of Smith.
2. Ricardo is Smith's only *rival.*

3. The population would be subject only to the *repeated* and *terrible deprivations* imposed by famine or by war.
4. Ricardo, like Malthus, *imagined* a constant growth in population.
5. It was man's *destiny*.
6. Labor *fixed* the value of things.
7. In Ricardo's system, the main figure was still the *proprietor*.
8. Smith and Ricardo disagreed over the question of the *high income* enjoyed by the proprietors.
9. There could be a lack of *buying power*.
10. The most urgent duty of government was to offset the *lack* of purchasing power.

(B) Fill in the blanks with the words listed below

Comparative Advantage

produce / less / export / advantage / cloth / advantage / similar / concluded / efficiently / example / import / observed / import / export / advantage / had

Ricardo ....(1) that in cases ....(2) to ours, while the United States had an absolute ....(3) over Britain in both wheat and ....(4), it had a greater advantage in wheat than in cloth. He ....(5) that a country would ....(6) the product in which it had the greater ....(7), or a comparative ....(8) and ....(9) the commodity in which its disadvantage was ....(10), or in which it ....(11) a comparative disadvantage. In this ....(12) the United States would ....(13) wheat and ....(14) cloth, even though it could ....(15) cloth more ....(16) than Britain.

◇ EXERCISE 3 ***Grammar***

Already / always / yet / still

Complete the sentences using the correct adverb

1. Say's Law states that a given level of output will .... generate an amount of income equal to that output.
2. Say and Ricardo .... ruled supreme at the onset of the Great Depression.
3. By the latter half of the nineteenth century Marx had .... transformed the labor theory of value into a revolutionary proposal.
4. People .... believe that the assembly line is a twentieth century concept.
5. Until Keynes, Malthus's idea of a shortage of purchasing power had not .... become accepted doctrine.
6. Rich countries have almost .... developed on the basis of tariff protection and subsidies.
7. Enormous pressures have been exerted on developing countries to adopt free trade, but many have chosen not to deregulate their economies ....
8. Over the past two decades a marked slowdown has .... occurred in the growth of the developing countries.
9. Despite the advice of the IMF, the World Bank and the WTO, many developing countries .... face economic failure.
10. The international investment community has .... tried to get developing countries to adopt "best-practice" institutions such as strong patent laws.

DEBATE

FREE TRADE

History debunks myth that free trade is best for all

◇ EXERCISE

Read the article below and discuss or write answers to the following questions

1. Why did Adam Smith tell Americans that they should not protect their industries?
2. Did Ulysses Grant believe in free trade?
3. Is there something hypocritical today about demanding that developing countries practise free trade?
4. Have developed countries' prescriptions for poorer countries been successful?
5. Do the author's recommendations allow for hope?

History debunks myth that free trade is best for all

You are visiting a developing country as a policy analyst. It has the highest average tariff rate in the world. Most of the population cannot vote, and vote-buying and electoral fraud are widespread.

The country has never recruited a single civil servant through an open process. Its public finances are precarious, with loan defaults that worry investors. It has no competition law, has abolished its shambolic bankruptcy law, and does not acknowledge foreigners' copyrights. In short, it is doing everything against the advice of the IMF, the World Bank, the World Trade Organisation and the international investment community.

Sounds like a recipe for development disaster? But no. The country is the United States – only that the time is around 1880, when its income level was similar to that of Morocco and Indonesia today. Despite wrong policies and sub-standard institutions, it was then one of the fastestgrowing – and rapidly becoming one of the richest – countries in the world.

Especially in relation to trade policy. Many top economists, including Adam Smith, had been telling Americans for over a century that they should not protect their industries – exactly what today's development orthodoxy tells developing countries.

But the Americans knew exactly what the game was. Many knew all too clearly that Britain, which was preaching free trade to their country, became rich on the basis of protectionism and subsidies. Ulysses Grant, the civil war hero who was president between 1868 and 1876, remarked that "within 200 years, when America has gotten out of protection all that it can offer, it too will adopt free trade". How prescient – except that his country did rather better than his prediction.

The fact is that rich countries did not develop on the basis of the policies and institutions they now recommend to developing countries. Virtually all of them used tariff protection and subsidies to develop their industries.

Once they became rich, these countries started demanding that the poorer countries practise free trade and introduce "advanced" institutions – if necessary through colonialism and unequal treaties. Friedrich List, the leading German economist of the mid-19th century, argued that in this way the more developed countries wanted to "kick away the ladder" with which they climbed to the top and so deny poorer countries the chance to develop.

In the past two decades developed countries have exerted enormous pressures on developing countries to adopt free trade, deregulate their economies, open their capital markets, and adopt "best-practice" institutions such as strong patent laws.

During this period, a marked slowdown has occurred in the growth of the developing countries. How do we address this failure?

First, the conditions attached to bilateral and multilateral financial assistance to developing countries should be radically changed. It should be accepted that the orthodox recipe is not working, and also that there can be no "best-practice" policies that everyone should use.

Second, the WTO rules should be rewritten so that the developing countries can more actively use tariffs and subsidies for development.

Third, improvements in institutions should be encouraged, but this should not be equated with imposing a fixed set of Anglo-American institutions on all countries, nor should it be attempted in haste, as institutional development is a lengthy and costly process.

By being allowed to adopt policies and institutions that are more suitable to their conditions, the developing countries will be able to develop faster. This will also benefit the developed countries in the long run, as it will increase their trade and investment opportunities. That the developed countries cannot see this is the tragedy of our time.

Ha-Joon Chang*, *Guardian Weekly*, 27 June 2002 (p.14)

* Ha-Joon Chang teaches at the University of Cambridge.

CHAPTER 5

MARX: THE PRODUCTION OF SURPLUS VALUE

◇ Key words and concepts

product
use value
commodities
means of production
labour power
money
market
surplus value
labour
labourer
prevent
exchange value
sustenance

◇ Vocabulary aid

yarn	fil
injury	préjudice

Instructions For Study

1° Turn to the **definitions** following the text *Marx: The Production of Surplus Value*. They refer to the specialist terms printed in **bold** type in the list of **Key words and concepts.** Study them closely and pinpoint them in the text.
2° Use an **English** language dictionary to check the meanings (in context) of the other words in the list.
3° Do the exercises to test your comprehension, vocabulary and grammar skills.

Marx: The Production of Surplus Value

The product appropriated by the capitalist is a use-value, as yarn, for example, or boots. But, although boots are, in one sense, the basis of all social progress, and our capitalist is a decided "progressist," yet he does not manufacture boots for their own sake. Use-value is, by no means, the thing "qu'on aime pour lui-même" in the production of commodities.

Our capitalist has two objects in view: in the first place, he wants to produce a use-value that has a value in exchange, that is to say, an article destined to be sold, a commodity; and secondly, he desires to produce a commodity whose value shall be greater than the sum of the values of the commodities used in its production, that is, of the means of production and the labour-power, that he purchased with his good money in the open market. His aim is to produce not only a use-value, but a commodity also; not only use-value, but value; not only value, but at the same time surplus-value.

The fact that half a day's labour is necessary to keep the labourer alive during 24 hours, does not in any way prevent him from working a whole day. Therefore, the value of labour-power, and the value which that labour-power creates in the labour-process, are two entirely different magnitudes; and this difference of the two values was what the capitalist had in view, when he was purchasing the labour-power. The useful qualities that labour-power possesses, and by virtue of which it makes yarn or boots, were to him nothing more than a *conditio sine qua non;* for in order to create value, labour must be expended in a useful manner. What really influenced him was the specific use-value which this commodity possesses of being *a source not only of value, but of more value than it has itself.* This is the special service that the capitalist expects from labour-power, and in this transaction he acts in accordance with the "eternal laws" of the exchange of commodities. The seller of labour-power, like the seller of any other commodity, realises its exchange-value, and parts with its use-value. He cannot take the one without giving the other. The use-value of labour-power, or in other words, labour, belongs just a little to its seller, as the use-value of oil after it has been sold belongs to the dealer who has sold it. The owner of the money has paid the value of a day's labour-power; his, therefore, is the use of it for a day; a day's labour belongs to him. The circumstance, that on the one hand the daily sustenance of labour-power costs only half a day's labour, while on the other hand the very same labour-power can work during a whole day, that consequently the value which its use during one day creates, is double what he pays for that use, this circumstance is, without doubt, a piece of good luck for the buyer, but by no means an injury to the seller.

K. Marx, *Capital,* Vol 1, VII, 1867, London: Lawrence &Wishart, 1954 (pp.181, 187-188)

◇◇ DEFINITIONS ◇◇◇

- **product** goods produced, output
- **use value** all the characteristics of a product which enable people to derive utility from it
- **commodities** economic goods
- **means of production** the physical aspects of capital (factories, tools, machinery and partly processed raw materials)
- **labour power** the worker's ability or capacity to produce
- **money** a customary medium of exchange, used as a unit of account and as a means for storing value
- **market** a place where goods and services are sold
- **surplus value** the difference between the worker's use value to the capitalist who employs him and the exchange value of his labour, i.e. between the value which is created by the worker and that which is paid to him
- **labour** human element of the production process; *work*
- **exchange value** the quantity of other commodities (or the quantity of money) for which a commodity will exchange on the market (determined by the amount of labour embodied in a product, i.e. used up in its manufacture)

◇◇ EXERCISES ◇◇◇

◇ EXERCISE 1 *Comprehension*

True / False Circle the correct choice and justify your answer

1. The capitalist manufactures boots only for their use value and exchange value. T / F
2. Two different values can be attributed to labour power. T / F
3. Marx believed labour power was a commodity. T / F
4. The worker is paid for both the use value and the exchange value of his labour. T / F
5. The worker creates more value than is necessary for his upkeep. T / F

◇ EXERCISE 2 *Vocabulary*

Use the list of definitions above to **select the appropriate term** to fit each sentence

1. At the end of one hour's spinning, a definite quantity of yarn, in other words, a definite quantity of ...., has become embodied in the cotton.
2. The value of ...., and the value which that labour-power creates in the labour-process, are two entirely different magnitudes.
3. The value of a product is merely the sum of the values of the .... that were thrown into the process of production.

4. In the making of jewellery, just as in spinning, the .... results only from a quantitative excess of labour.
5. By turning his .... into commodities that serve as the material elements of a new product, the capitalist at the same time converts value into capital.

◇ EXERCISE 3 *Grammar*

Tenses

Complete the following paragraph with the correct form of the verb in brackets

Marx (*to develop*) (1) from Adam Smith and David Ricardo their labour theory of value, which (*to hold*) (2) the central place in his economic theory. For Ricardo, the amount of labour used in the production of commodities (*to be*) (3) a rough determinant of relative prices in the long run. For Marx, however, the quantity of labour used up in the manufacture of a product (*to determine*) (4) value, and this value (*to be*) (5) fundamental and immutable. He (*to do*) (6) not satisfactorily (*to explain*) (7) any connection with relative prices. Labour consumption (*to determine*) (8) exchange value, which (*to differ*) (9) from use value. The distinction between the two in the case of labour, regarded in itself as a commodity, (*to be*) (10) a vital one in Marx's analysis. The capitalist (*to pay*) (11) wages which (*to be*) (12) determined by the exchange value of workers. This exchange value (*to be*) (13), in turn, determined by the socially necessary labour time required to "produce" the worker, that (*to be*) (14) the labour inputs required (*to rear*) (15), (*to feed*) (16), (*to clothe*) (17) and (*to educate*) (18) him. However, in return the capitalist (*to get*) (19) the labourer's use value. The value of the labourer to the capitalist who (*to use*) (20) him (*to be*) (21) greater than the value the capitalist paid in exchange for his services. This difference Marx (*to call*) (22) "surplus value".

FROM THE NEWS

LABOUR COSTS

Mexican workers pay for their success

◇ EXERCISE

Read the article below and discuss or write answers to the following questions

1. How is the globalized economy at work?
2. What effect did NAFTA have?
3. How is Mexican industry responding?
4. Why does Mexico still have an advantage in some product lines?
5. Is the TV capital doomed?

Mexican workers pay for their success

TIJUANA, Mexico: Cesiah Ruiz Brena came to Tijuana in 1989, deliriously happy to get a job at a new Japanese factory. Her work space was grand, the lights were bright and the pay was unimaginably good: $100 a week to start.

But after 13 years during which her wages rose to $200 a week, Ruiz Brena lost her job on June 1. Her Canon inkjet printer factory shut down. She and her co-workers shared a cake, snapped photos of one another and said goodbye. The factory, they were told, was moving to Thailand and Vietnam, where wages are as low as $15 a week – less than what she earns in a day.

All along the Mexican border with the United States, once-busy factories are closing. Since the end of 2000, tearful farewell parties have been held for 250,000 factory workers in Mexico. Some of the same jobs that have left North Carolina textile plants and Ohio auto-parts assembly lines for Mexico in the 1980s are now moving to Asia. The reason is the same: cheaper labor.

The loss of jobs in part reflects the slowdown in the U.S. economy. But many of the plant closings are just the globalized economy at work. Factories came to take advantage of low wages; now that success has driven wages up, they are moving on. Mexico is left with a bittersweet legacy: higher wages, but fewer jobs.

More than 500 foreign-owned assembly-line factories in Mexico, called *maquiladoras*, have closed in the past two years, in part because wages have doubled in the past 10 years and are no longer considered low in the world economy. An entry-level factory worker in Tijuana earns $1.50 to $2 an hour, compared with 25 cents an hour in parts of China.

International companies once wary of China are increasingly inclined to invest there. Those include a golf-club manufacturer that laid off 1,500 employees in Tijuana and an electronics factory in Guadalajara that left 4,000 workers jobless when it moved. Suddenly Mexican workers feel that China is their fiercest competitor, sucking their jobs east.

"It's a reality of globalization," said a Mexican economist, Rogelio Ramirez de la O. As he surveys companies in Mexico, he said, talk is increasingly of moving to China.

"This is not going to turn around automatically," he said. "It's a structural adjustment in the world economy."

The factory closures are a jolt to an industry that until 2001 had never known a year in which it did not grow. Started in the mid-1960s, the factories had been expanding steadily, with double-digit annual growth after passage of the North American Free Trade Agreement, or NAFTA, in 1994. The pact meant that designer jeans could be sewn and television sets assembled in Mexico cheaply, then shipped tax-free to the United States, the world's largest consumer.

From 120 export factories in 1970, the industry swelled to more than 3,700 in 2000. In Tijuana, a border city of 1.5 million residents just south of San Diego, one new industrial park after another opened over the last 15 years. Today, sprawling electronics, auto- and medical-supply factories ring the city. The maquiladora industry produces half of Mexico's $143 billion annual exports of manufactured goods.

But in responding to the new reality of overseas competition, the industry is trying to shift from labor-intensive assembly, in which China and other Asian countries now have the edge, toward higher-skilled, higher-tech manufacturing. As a result, the number of factories has receded to about 3,200.

"It's similar to the reinventing that had to be done in the United States" in the 1980s, said Ramirez de la O.

But, he said, Mexico is ill-prepared for the transition. The government has been lax about monitoring wage increases and supporting worker education and training programs, preferring to believe that the factory problems will disappear with the U.S. recession. "That has clouded their eyes to the problems," he said.

Wages in Mexico have risen faster than inflation, and faster than those in the United States and Asia. Rolando Gonzalez, president of the National Maquiladora Association, said that is not all bad. Fatter salaries mean better housing and better living conditions for workers, he said, and Asian competition is forcing an improvement in workers' skills.

In what many see as a harbinger, Pratt & Whitney just opened an aircraft parts repair factory, locating its hightech operation in what was once a low-tech Styrofoam packing plant.

"Times are changing," said Tijuana's mayor, Jose de Jesus Gonzalez Reyes. "Companies used to come here for our low-cost labor. That is not our best selling point anymore."

The mayor said a natural evolution is taking place: Over time workers do better, more difficult work and, therefore, earn more money. Now, rather than promoting Tijuana as a hub of cheap labor, Gonzalez said, the city is focusing on its location next to the United States.

"This is our new strategy, selling the Tijuana-San Diego region," he said.

It is cheaper to truck most goods from Mexico to the United States than to ship them from Asia. But the wage differential between China and Mexico is so great that the bottom line usually tips to production in China.

Still, for some large items that are the most costly to transport, such as automobiles, Mexico has an advantage. Toyota recently announced plans to open a new pickup truckbed factory.

Tijuana has a long history of reinventing itself to respond to economic changes. In the 1980s, the city took advantage of a pre-NAFTA free trade zone to create what many called the "perfume capital of the world". Companies imported perfumes from Europe, then took advantage of free trade benefits to sell them duty-free to large U.S. retailers.

When NAFTA provided tax-free incentives for maquiladoras, Tijuana subsituted perfume bottles for crates of electronics components and became one of the world's leading television assembly sites.

But Asian manufacturers have made steady inroads into Tijuana's television territory. "If we don't want to lose the title of TV capital, we need to get into plasma and high-definition TV," said Humberto Inzunza Fonseca, Tijuana's director of economic development. "We are in the process of changing again."

Mary Jordan, © 2002, *The Washington Post*,
Reprinted with permission.

KEYNES: SAVING AND GROWTH

◇ Key words and concepts

saving
growth
thrift
full employment
assuming
claim
demand
supply
depression
unemployed
recession
investment
inventory
pileups
opportunities
paradox of thrift
effective demand
propensity to save
consumer
output
income
benefit
full use of capacity
actual
hoard
eventually
spending
raise
unused capacity
available
outlets

Instructions For Study

1° Turn to the **definitions** following the text *Keynes: Saving and Growth*. They refer to the specialist terms printed in **bold** type in the list of **Key words and concepts.** Study them closely and pinpoint them in the text.
2° Use an **English** language dictionary to check the meanings (in context) of the other words in the list.
3° Do the exercises to test your comprehension, vocabulary and grammar skills.

Keynes: Saving and Growth

Keynes challenged the classical conclusions about saving and growth. He argued that more thrift and saving lead to more rapid economic growth *only if full employment is assumed*. This means assuming the classical claim that demand is always enough for any supply of goods and that all saving is automatically invested. This assumption, however, is *not* true according to Keynes. During each depression it is painfully obvious to everyone that there is not full employment and that millions of workers are involuntarily unemployed. In each recession or depression, most saving is not being invested (except in the statistical sense of investment in unplanned and unwanted inventory pileups).

Keynes showed that, with unemployment and lack of investment opportunities, more saving may actually lead to *less* production rather than any economic growth. This finding constitutes the Alice-in-Wonderland theme of the *paradox of thrift*, which says that greater thrift and saving may sometimes lead to less output, not more. If the economy is faced with a lack of effective demand, then a higher propensity to save will simply lower consumer demand still further. The lower consumer demand may then lead to still less output and income, and therefore, to less aggregate saving and investment than there was before individuals tried to save more of their income. Thrift may always be an individual virtue, as Benjamin Franklin preached, but it is not always a social virtue when there is a lack of paying customers in a private enterprise economy.

More saving at a given income level is a benefit to the economy if, and only if, there is an equal increase in investment. Therefore, Keynesians see the potential growth rate as *only* a potential, a possibility that will be realized only if all saving really is invested and becomes an increase in capital. So all of the above model of growth should really be restated in terms of potential output at full use of capacity (Z), not in terms of actual output (Y), because there may be insufficient effective demand. In other words, more saving, which could supply more capital to produce more output, is helpful only if business people expect demand to rise by an equal amount. If they do not expect an increase in demand, they will hoard the increased saving and precipitate a recession or depression. Domar emphasized that new investment does eventually increase supply as well as demand. So the condition for steady growth is not merely no hoarding of present income, but also an increase of income and spending proportionate to growth of supply. If demand does not increase in the required amount, then the economy leaves the golden path of steady growth and may never return to it.

In the modern world, neither side of the problem can be ignored. Setting aside more saving to invest in more capital makes it *possible* to raise the rate of growth. But this happy possibility cannot become a reality as long as significant numbers of unemployed persons and unused capacity continue. Such conditions show that all the savings now available are not being invested. More saving would only cause more unemployment in this case. First, one must guarantee a solution to the Keynesian problem of finding profitable investment outlets for all existing savings. Then one can worry about the classical problem of generating a higher rate of saving to allow the possibility of more investment.

Howard J. Sherman & Gary R. Evans, *Macroeconomics*,
New York: Harper & Row, 1984 (pp.229-230)

◇◇ DEFINITIONS ◇◇◇

- ♦**saving** postponing current consumption to accumulate wealth
- ♦**growth** an increase in a nation's output of goods and services over time
- ♦**thrift** careful management of money, avoiding waste
- ♦**full employment** situation in which all persons willing and able to work can find a job at current rates of pay
- ♦**demand** quantity of a good that will be bought at a given price at a given time
- ♦**supply** quantity of a good available on the market at a given time
- ♦**depression** a large and persistent fall in the level of output and employment
- ♦**recession** a slowdown in economic activity; *slump*
- ♦**investment** expenditure on assets with the purpose of obtaining a return
- ♦**inventory** a detailed list of goods for sale, showing quantities and values; *stock on hand*
- ♦**paradox of thrift** an increase in savings may sometimes lead to lower national income
- ♦**effective demand** demand for goods backed up by purchasing power (the ability to pay)
- ♦**propensity to save** the ratio of total saving to total income
- ♦**consumer** buyer of goods who uses them to satisfy his needs
- ♦**output** the total goods produced
- ♦**income** the return on the use of land, labor or capital; *earnings*
- ♦**full use of capacity** maximum level of output attainable by using fully present machinery
- ♦**hoard** to accumulate deliberately beyond normal needs
- ♦**unused capacity** the difference between actual output and output at full productive capacity; *excess capacity, idle capacity* or *spare capacity*

◇◇ EXERCISES ◇◇◇

◇ EXERCISE 1 *Comprehension*

Circle the alternative (a), (b) or (c) that most fully and correctly completes the statement

1. Keynes considered that further saving will increase growth
   (a) if it is reinvested
   (b) if demand is high enough
   (c) only in a situation of full employment

2. The paradox of thrift consists in saying that
   (a) more thrift may sometimes lower output
   (b) more saving tends to increase production
   (c) supply will usually match demand

3. According to Keynesians, if all saving is actually invested
   (a) the economy will slow down
   (b) demand will decrease
   (c) growth is possible

4. The condition for regular growth
   (a) is to spend as much as possible
   (b) avoiding excessive saving consistent with an increase of income and spending proportionate to growth of supply
   (c) is to invest continually in more capital

5. In a context of high unemployment
   (a) more thrift will decrease demand
   (b) more saving will increase the number of jobless people
   (c) growth can only be achieved through saving

◇ EXERCISE 2 *Vocabulary*

Fill in the blanks with the words listed below

wage / increase / lend / would / drop / prices / value / interest / theory / real / deny / investment / money

Keynes did not ....(1) the classical ....(2). He agreed that a reduction in ....(3) rates could, in theory, be beneficial, but it ....(4) operate only through the liquidity preference schedule. A fall in ....(5) would increase the ....(6) of ....(7) in people's hands in ....(8) terms. This would make available an ....(9) in the amount that people were willing to ....(10) with a consequent ....(11) in the rate of ....(12) to the benefit of ....(13).

◇ EXERCISE 3 *Grammar*

Do or make?

Fill in the blanks using the appropriate form of the verb

1. Keynes .... his best to draw a sharp distinction between saving and investing.
2. According to Keynes, economists would be .... a mistake if they believed that all saving was being invested.
3. In the period between the two world wars, little was .... to alleviate 'poverty in the midst of plenty'.
4. Saving means .... the choice to spend less on consumption.
5. Entrepreneurs will be unable to .... sufficient business if there is a lack of paying customers.
6. Keynes urged the government to .... its duty by compensating for the shortage of purchasing power.
7. The government will need to .... urgent arrangements to fund public works projects.
8. When there is a lack of investment opportunities, ... profits may well be postponed.

PART C

POLITICAL ECONOMY

IN THIS PART YOU WILL READ ABOUT

- The role of the stock exchange
- The trials and tribulations of the FTSE 100 index
- Basic economic exchange
- Barter companies
- The standard of living
- Trade and protectionism

YOU WILL LEARN SOME BASIC ECONOMIC TERMS CONCERNING

- Shareholding and investment
- Stock markets
- Money and exchange
- Living standards
- Output figures
- Terms of trade

CHAPTER 6

THE STOCK EXCHANGE

◇ Key words and concepts

stock exchange
securities
dealt in
second hand
finance
embodied
earning capacity
firm
committed to
owner
business
wealth
investments
convenience
rentiers
issues
performs
liquidity
interest
dividends
retention of profits
limited liability
peculiar
managers
amortization funds
net profit
growth
productive capacity
shareholders
provided that
earnings
share
designers
drop into the lap of
grant
return
endowed
provision

Instructions For Study

1° Turn to the **definitions** following the text *The Stock Exchange*. They refer to the specialist terms printed in **bold** type in the list of **Key words and concepts.** Study them closely and pinpoint them in the text.
2° Use an **English** language dictionary to check the meanings (in context) of the other words in the list.
3° Do the exercises to test your comprehension, vocabulary and grammar skills.

The Stock Exchange

A stock exchange is a market in which securities can be dealt in at second hand. The finance that they represent was long ago expended by government, or embodied in earning capacity by a firm. A firm is committed to some particular line of activity. The securities can pass from one owner to another every day, without having any effect on the business that they represent. Securities, therefore, are a much more liquid form of wealth than real investments.

The Stock Exchange is primarily a convenience for rentiers. A large and well-paid profession has grown up in the business of dealing in second-hand securities. New issues are initially dealt with by specialist institutions. But, indirectly, the Stock Exchange performs a service to industry, making securities attractive by increasing their liquidity and so keeping down the cost (in terms of interest and dividends) of raising finance. For established companies, however, the main source of finance for new investment is retention of profits. The amount of new finance that passes through a stock exchange is very small compared to the great volume of dealings at second hand.

As a result of the system of limited liability, retention of profits has led to a peculiar system of property. The managers of firms are continually reinvesting amortization funds in new equipment, and they also retain a large proportion of net profit to finance the growth of their productive capacity. All the new capital which is created in this way legally belongs to the shareholders. Provided that the investments are successful, the flow of earnings corresponding to a share is continually rising; the stock-exchange value of the share goes up correspondingly. Thus, the wealth created by the workers, managers, and designers employed by the firms is dropping into the laps of the rentiers without their contributing anything to production. As Professor Galbraith has pointed out: “No grant of feudal privilege has ever equalled, for effortless return, that of the grandparent who bought and endowed his descendants with a thousand shares of General Motors or General Electric”. The main economic role of a stock exchange is the preservation and expansion of rentier wealth, rather than the provision of finance for industry or government.

Joan Robinson & John Eatwell, *An Introduction to Modern Economics*,
London: Mc Graw-Hill, 1973 (pp.225-226)

◇◇ DEFINITIONS ◇◇◇

- **stock exchange** a place where stocks and shares are bought and sold (traded)
- **securities** stocks, shares and bonds
- **finance** a supply of money; *funds*
- **firm** a business organization; *business, business concern, enterprise, company*
- **owner** the person to whom property belongs by right
- **business** commercial activity
- **wealth** the value of what is owned (assets); *riches*
- **investments** expenditure on assets (property) aimed at returning an income
- **rentiers** persons who live off a fixed income from land, stocks or bonds
- **issues** amounts of stock placed in circulation by a company at a particular time
- **liquidity** the relative ease with which something of value (assets) can be converted into cash
- **interest** a sum of money paid for the use of capital, usually expressed as a rate or percentage
- **dividends** payments to the shareholders of a company on the basis of profits earned
- **retention of profits** retained earnings , non-distributed earnings of a company
- **limited liability** shareholders have no legal obligation to settle any debts incurred by a company beyond the extent of their investment (shareholding) in it
- **manager** person employed to run an organization, having decision-making or supervisory responsibilities
- **amortization funds** money held by a firm to pay off the debts incurred to buy machinery or equipment; *sinking funds*
- **net profit** the profit remaining after deducting all selling expenses and operating costs from the gross profit of an enterprise
- **productive capacity** plant, machinery and equipment
- **shareholders** owners of stock in a corporation; *stockholder; stakeholder*
- **earnings** the income accruing to the enterprise; *profits*
- **share** a part or portion of the (equity) capital of a company; *stock*
- **return** the actual rate of monetary return on an investment

◇◇ EXERCISES ◇◇◇

◇ EXERCISE 1 *Comprehension*

Answer these questions

1. What is the nature of the comparison with "real investments"?
2. What service does the Stock Exchange render industry?
3. Why do managers reinvest amortization funds in new equipment?
4. How does the value of a share go up?
5. What point is Professor Galbraith making?

◇ EXERCISE 2 *Vocabulary*

(A) Use the list of definitions above to **select the appropriate terms** to fit each sentence

1. As a result of the principle of ...., if a business goes bankrupt and cannot pay its creditors, its .... become worthless but a shareholder has no further obligation.
2. There are two main classes of business ....: shares which give a claim on the profits of the ...., and bonds which represent an acknowledgement of debt.
3. The need to pay out a .... – a share of net profit – is not very different from the need to pay .... on bonds.
4. When there is a rise in the level of .... , expectations of earnings per share have gone up.
5. Legally, the .... collectively own the capital of the business, but they are not .... in the full sense that they are responsible for the debts of the business.

(B) Select the verbs in the left-hand column which **match** the nouns in the right-hand column

1. to deal in	a) liquidity
2. to perform	b) finance
3. to increase	c) net profit
4. to keep down	d) a service
5. to raise	e) growth
6. to reinvest	f) funds
7. to retain	g) securities
8. to finance	h) the cost

◇ EXERCISE 3 *Grammar*

Passive and Active Voice

(A) Rewrite these sentences in the **passive voice**

1. The NYSE is going to launch a new stock index.
2. Wall Street has taken another step towards electronic trading.
3. The bank is developing a long term strategy.
4. We are creating an exchange that is far more efficient.
5. The trend is already transforming many markets in Asia.

(B) Rewrite these sentences in the **active voice**, using the subject provided in brackets

1. A Stock Exchange is a market in which securities are traded. (stockbrokers)
2. New bonds were issued last month. (the government)
3. There have been complaints about the high cost of transactions. (market analysts)
4. The market value of shares is expected to increase. (equity holders)
5. The Dow Jones Industrial Average is considered to be one of the most useful market guides. (many investors)

FROM THE BUSINESS NEWS

2002 "ANNUS HORRIBILIS"

Footsie year full of false dawns

◇ EXERCISE

Read the article below and discuss or write answers to the following questions

1. What sort of a year was 2002 for the FTSE 100 index?
2. How did UK insurers affect the market?
3. Which sectors fared well in the UK stock market?
4. Describe some of the major casualties.
5. What explanation is given for the market's woes in 2002?

Footsie year full of false dawns

Faulty forescasts

FTSE 100 index

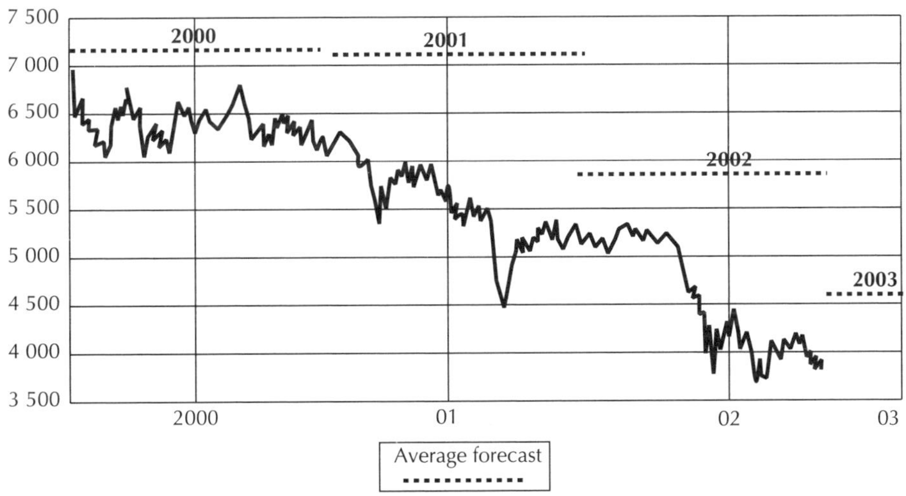

The London Stock Exchange's main index has suffered its third-biggest fall in the past 200 years with hopes of an end to the bear market frequently dashed. Hard-pressed investors may be facing more tough times ahead.

The past year has truly been an "annus horribilis" for UK equity investors, with the FTSE 100 index of leading shares suffering its third-biggest fall in the past 200 years.

The FTSE 100 has fallen by almost a quarter from 5,217.4 to 3,940.40.

This made 2002 the worst year for UK equities since 1974 when the market fell 55 per cent in one year.

It also marked a third year of falling values for the first time in 40 years when the decline was much smaller.

But it was also a year of false hopes, as analysts desperately alighted on any short period of share price strength to herald the end of the bear market.

These included the two-month uptick over the summer and another six-week respite in October-November.

Investors' hopes for the end of the downturn were dashed, however, and the market ended the year with little optimism remaining.

The FTSE 100 index also experienced its greatest levels of volatility since it was created.

Investors became frustrated as share prices moved by 10 per cent in a day for little apparent reason.

One of the forces behind the extreme levels of volatility, and the shortlived nature of any market rally, has been the pressure on insurers and large institutional investors to sell into any strength in price.

UK insurers have long been conscious that their equity holdings were too high, making them aware of the need to shift more assets out of shares.

But many were reluctant to sell at what they perceived to be the bottom of the market. That led to sales pressure as soon as prices picked up.

Some insurers also became forced sellers as the fall in equity prices threatened their solvency levels.

Equitable Life, the beleaguered life assurer, revealed in November it had sold £2bn in equities, cutting its holdings to "negligible" levels.

The pressure on the insurers' bottom lines, also affected the wider market: Aviva, formerly CGNU, cut its dividend by 40 per cent and Legal & General launched a £786m rights issue in September to bolster its capital.

Royal & Sun Alliance also saw its share price knocked and ousted its chief executive.

The weakness in insurance and financial stocks cast a shadow over the rest of the index which is heavily weighted towards these types of company.

In fact, only two sectors in the UK stock market have shown positive returns this year – the tobacco sub-group showed a 20.1 per cent increase in price over the year and personal care and household products enjoyed a similar bounce.

This was reflected in the best performing shares of the year, which were Imperial Tobacco with a rise of 39 per cent and Gallaher group, another tobacco company, which increased by 31 per cent.

Reckitt Benckiser, the household products group was the third-best performer, rising 20 per cent.

But traditional defensive sectors such as utilities and food producers all suffered an overall decline in price – by 6 per cent and 1 per cent respectively.

There have also been some spectacular falls from grace of individual stocks. For example, Marconi – the telecommunications equipment group and stalwart of many personal portfolios – has seen its share price all but disappear.

The price has fallen by 96 per cent this year and after leaving the FTSE 100 in September 2001, it was ejected from the FTSE 250 in June.

Other high-profile casualties of the FTSE 100 include Cable and Wireless, the telecoms company – the worst performer in the index and recently ejected after its share price fell 86 per cent.

Reuters, the news information group, was the second-worst performer as the downturn hit its clients in the City and its share price fell 74 per cent.

Only 16 of the stocks that were in the FTSE 100 at the beginning of the year have gone up in price and four of these were acquired, according to Schroder Salomon Smith Barney.

British Airways – one of Britain's highest profile companies – suffered an ignominious elimination from the FTSE 100 in September but was reinstated on December 23.

Corus, the steelmaker, and Brambles Industries were not so lucky and were thrown out of the blue chip index at the end of the year.

Much of the decline in the FTSE 100 came in the third quarter when the market suffered its biggest quarterly loss since the crash of 1987.

The index reached its lowest point for the year on September 24 when it hit an intra-day low of 3,609 to close at 3,671.

The gloom that beset the market in 2002 came against a background of a fairly benign economy.

But economists point to an imbalance in demand, with consumers and the public sector providing the main support.

Fears for this year centre on a downturn in the housing market and high levels of consumer debt as well as the possibility of a prolonged conflict with Iraq.

Hard-pressed UK investors can see little relief on the horizon.

Deborah Hargreaves, *Financial Times*, 2 January 2003 (p.14)

CHAPTER 7

BARTER AND MONEY

◇ Key words and concepts

barter
goods
pedlar
currency system
eventually
wants
items
overcome
holding over
trust
sorting out
worth
carry over
discarded
store
deferred
claim
yield
achieved
valuable
coinage metals
token
law-making
legal tender
fair
price
save up
afford
debts
businesses
record
instalment
taxes
rates
inconvenient

◇ Vocabulary aid

to weave	tisser
cloth	tissu
axe	hache
plump	dodu
wheat	blé
riot	émeute

Instructions For Study

1° Turn to the **definitions** following the text *Barter and Money*. They refer to the specialist terms printed in **bold** type in the list of **Key words and concepts.** Study them closely and pinpoint them in the text.
2° Use an **English** language dictionary to check the meanings (in context) of the other words in the list.
3° Do the exercises to test your comprehension, vocabulary and grammar skills.

Barter and Money

Exchange by Barter

Until a full money system has been developed, trade is usually carried on by barter. This is the exchange of goods directly for other goods, and it presents quite serious problems to the parties trading. These problems are not a real handicap when trading is an unusual event, for example in simple tribal societies practising autarchy (self-sufficiency). To people growing their own food, keeping their own cattle and weaving their own cloth, the occasional bartering activity can usually be resolved fairly easily. The purchase of a knife or an axe, at an annual fair, or from the visiting pedlar, is an event to which due time can be given.

When we live in a community where specialization is the rule, so that every single thing we need has to be obtained by exchange, the difficulties of barter become so onerous that a 'money' system has to be developed.

Even today it is sometimes necessary to use barter. The collapse of a currency system, such as occurred in Germany at the end of the Second World War, meant that barter took place on an extensive scale, and eventually cigarettes acted as money.

The Disadvantages of Barter

The disadvantages of barter are (*a*) the need for a coincidence of wants, (*b*) the difficulty of deciding equal values, and (*c*) the indivisibility of large items.

(*a*) *The necessity for a coincidence of wants.* It is impossible to barter unless *A* has what *B* wants, and *A* wants what *B* has. Sometimes this difficulty can be overcome by holding one half of the transaction over until a later time, but this requires trust and a sense of honouring obligations. It is made easier if the respective parties can read and write, so that the debt can be recorded. The records of citizens of the early United States include many such entries. Independence had ended the use of British currency before the United States was ready to provide a dollar system. 'I owe Nathanial Hawke 1 coil of rope length 20 yards', runs a typical entry.

(*b*) *The difficulty of deciding equal values.* Even when each party wants what the other has it does not follow they can agree on a fair exchange. Is a decorated pot worth a plump hen? A good deal of time can be wasted sorting out such equations of value.

(*c*) *The indivisibility of large items.* If a cow is worth two sacks of wheat, what is one sack of wheat worth? Once again we may need to carry over part of the transaction to a later period of time. This is not very easy even in a settled community; with nomadic peoples it is very difficult indeed.

For these reasons the barter system is discarded by societies which develop beyond autarky to more specialized methods of production. For such peoples a money system is essential.

The Functions of Money

Money is (*a*) medium of exchange, (*b*) a measure of value, (*c*) a store of value, (*d*) a standard for deferred payments, and (*e*) it facilitates one-way payments.

(*a*) *A medium of exchange.* This is the chief function of money. It overcomes the need for a coincidence of wants, since everyone 'wants' money, which represents a claim against any goods or services which will yield satisfaction. It does follow, though, that money must be generally acceptable. In earlier times this general acceptability was achieved by using metals which were themselves valuable: the coinage metals gold, silver, and copper. Today all coins are 'token' money only, that is they are acceptable because we all agree to accept them as being worth a certain claim against goods and services. This general acceptability is supported by a declaration by the law-making body that the tokens do constitute 'legal tender'.

(*b*) *A measure of value.* This function overcomes the difficulty of equating a decorated pot with a plump hen. We exchange the hen for what is agreed to be a fair quantity of money – now called the price of the hen. We then see whether it is sufficient money to buy the decorated pot. If it is not, we must save the price of the hen until we have enough other money to put with it to buy the pot. Thus the money is also useful as a store of value.

(*c*) *A store of value.* This store of value can also help us to overcome the disadvantage of barter, that some items are indivisible. The farmer with only one sack of wheat cannot buy half a cow, but he can save up the money he has obtained in exchange for his wheat in the hope that before long he will be able to afford a cow.

The use of money as a store of value only applies when individuals are storing it; a whole nation could not do so. Robinson Crusoe on his island found a box of gold coins which proved useless to him until he returned to civilization. If a whole nation stored up its money and then retired simultaneously they would all starve for lack of current production. Money is only a claim against the real goods and services which have utility. It is of no use unless the wealth is being created which yields satisfaction of wants.

(*d*) *A standard for deferred payments.* Money is a useful unit of account, and accounts are records of debts to businesses. It follows that the money system provides a standard for deferred payments, enabling us to record debts and eventually collect them either in one payment or in a series of payments on the instalment method. It is important here, however, that the value of money is stable over reasonably lengthy periods of time.

(*e*) *One-way payments*. Some payments are not made in exchange for goods or services directly enjoyed. The benefits of peaceful existence, freedom from riot and civil disturbance are enjoyed in return for one-way payments called taxes, or rates if they are levied locally. Such one-way payments are inconvenient without a money system.

Geoffrey Whitehead, *Economics*,
Oxford: Butterworth – Heinemann, 1996 (pp.165-167)

◇◇ DEFINITIONS ◇◇◇

- ♦ **barter** direct exchange of one good for another without the use of money
- ♦ **goods** tangible economic products that are used to satisfy human wants
- ♦ **currency system** a mechanism of exchange rate management between currencies
- ♦ **wants** the desires for commodities or services
- ♦ **claim** the right to make a demand for something
- ♦ **coinage metals** precious metals used to manufacture coins for use as money
- ♦ **legal tender** money which, by law, must be accepted in payment of a debt or obligation
- ♦ **price** value expressed in terms of money
- ♦ **debts** amounts of money owed by one party to another
- ♦ **businesses** firms, companies or other forms of enterprise
- ♦ **instalment** a partial payment of a debt
- ♦ **taxes** payments made to the legal authorities to meet public expenses
- ♦ **rates** taxes raised by local authorities according to a certain scale

◇◇ EXERCISES ◇◇◇

◇ EXERCISE 1 *Comprehension*

1. Money developed as a system of exchange because
   a) barter had become too widespread
   b) increasing specialization made direct trading difficult
   c) there were too few trade fairs

2. Barter was based on a philosophy of
   a) levelling people's wants
   b) the indivisibility of common economic goods
   c) fair exchange is no robbery

3. The chief advantage of money is
   a) it constitutes legal tender
   b) it increases people's wants
   c) it can defer payment for goods and services

4. Money functions as a measure of value which
   a) facilitates comparing unequal objects
   b) enables the recording of various transactions
   c) both of the above

5. Money is used as a store of value because
   a) it provides shelter from inflation
   b) it provides freedom from social unrest
   c) none of the above

◇ EXERCISE 2 *Vocabulary*

(A) Use the list of definitions above to **select the appropriate term** to fit each sentence

1. Originally money was in the form of coins, made from the ...., copper, silver and gold.
2. .... is any method of payment which we are forced by law to accept as adequate settlement of a debt.
3. Money is only a .... against the real goods and services which have utility.
4. The collapse of a currency system will lead .... to take place on an extensive scale.
5. Where devaluation of a .... is threatened, foreigners are unwilling to accept the notes or coinage of the country in question.

(B) Fill in the blanks using the words listed below

economic / economical / economy / economies / economics / Economist / economists / economically

1. In order to develop, market .... must be free from too many restrictions.
2. The .... is a famous British weekly magazine.
3. .... growth often leads to fiscal stimulus.
4. It is clear that these .... are proponents of globalization.
5. Reducing the army will be more ....
6. .... is not an exact science.
7. The government is looking for ways to apply this policy as .... as possible.
8. The Soviet .... was centrally planned.

◇ EXERCISE 3 *Grammar*

The **Infinitive** or the **Gerund**?

Choose between the **infinitive** (with or without **to**) and the **gerund**

1. Barter is carried out by (to trade / trade / trading) one commodity directly for another.
2. The chief function of money is (to serve / serve / serving) as a medium of exchange.
3. Developed societies need (to agree on / agree on / agreeing on) a convenient medium of exchange.
4. It was common among early tribal communities (to conduct / conduct / conducting) exchange by the barter system.
5. By developing metallic money early societies were able (to facilitate / facilitate / facilitating) exchange.
6. Modern bartering arrangements have made some Western suppliers (to rethink / rethink / rethinking) their export strategy.
7. Paper money constitutes a convenient way (to settle / settle / settling) a debt.
8. (to issue / issue / issuing) inconvertible paper money enabled governments to weather the monetary chaos following World War 1.

9. The treasurer's statement did nothing but (to confuse / confuse / confusing) bankers.
10. The government debated (to reduce / reduce / reducing) interest rates to boost the economy.

FROM THE NEWS

BARTER COMPANIES

Juicy stuff

◇ EXERCISE

Read the article below and discuss or write answers to the following questions

1. What are the prospects for barter companies?
2. What is meant by "challenging merchandise"?
3. What advantages do barter companies have over "close-out" companies?
4. How does Icon International make its money?

Juicy stuff

Making the most of an ancien business practice in a sagging economy

What do boned chicken breasts, rollerblades and sauerkraut juice have in common ? Answer: Icon International dabbles in these products and much else. Icon's business is barter, whose ancient skills remain surprisingly popular. Last year, barter companies traded $7.9 billion in goods and services worldwide, according to the International Reciprocal Trade Association (IRTA). Recession, thinks the IRTA, will boost that figure by more than 20% this year, as companies dump unsold stock.

Barter companies buy and sell the same sort of challenging merchandise as "close-out" companies, which buy ageing stock and sell it on to hospitals, prisons and other unconventional outlets. Typical deals include once-hot items for which demand has ended abruptly ("I'm real long on robotic dogs at the moment," says Icon's David Prose), or simply bad ideas, like the $2,000 lawnmowers painted in American football-team colours that Mr Prose has recently been trying to find a home for.

In part, barter experts are selling their remarketing skills. Manufacturers may have little or no control over where close-out companies offload their products. Icon, which has annual sales of $184m, works more closely with its clients. This might be important to owners of premium brands, who may not want last year's discounted gear on display with this year's full-priced stuff: Icon sells K2 Sports' old rollerblade models in Mexico and the Caribbean, not in America. But the big attraction of barter firms is price. Whereas close-out companies buy at a deep discount, Icon will pay the cost of production, or close to it. When it sells the product on, it is likely to recoup just one-third of that.

So how come it managed to make a profit of $24m before tax last year? Icon's secret is the currency in which it pays: so-called trade credits, which customers can exchange for business services, such as advertising and travel. Icon buys these services in advance, when it thinks that advertising space and airline tickets are cheap. The bet is that prices will rise, leaving Icon with a potential trading profit. These bets are then leveraged: in a typical deal, Icon sells three of four times as much in business services as it buys in goods, with customers paying in a mixture of trade credits and cash. And if Icon makes more on the advertising and airline-ticket trades than it loses on the sauerkraut juice, everybody wins-even if nobody will drink the stuff.

The Economist, 9 February 2002 (p.57)

CHAPTER 8

OUTPUT AND LIVING STANDARDS

◇ Key words and concepts

output
GDP
reliable
weightless
numbered
voluntary work
otherwise
tax
coping with
spills
crude oil
salvage
standard of living
assessed
national income
aware
growth
GNP
lie in
underground economy
recorded
shortening
current
pointless
average
per capita GDP
misleading
currencies
purchasing power
exchange rates

Instructions For Study

1° Turn to the **definitions** following the text *Output and Living Standards*. They refer to the specialist terms printed in **bold** type in the list of **Key words and concepts.** Study them closely and pinpoint them in the text.
2° Use an **English** language dictionary to check the meanings (in context) of the other words in the list.
3° Do the exercises to test your comprehension, vocabulary and grammar skills.

Output and Living Standards

Economists and statisticians complain increasingly that the traditional methods of calculating GDP are becoming less reliable. There are plenty of data on the production of coal, grain, and clothing, but useful data about today's fastest-growing industries – computing, telecommunications, business services, and finance – are much harder to find. Called by some the 'weightless economy', these activities cannot be seen and are not easily numbered.

Another deficiency is the exclusion of unpaid services from the figures. These 'non-market' activities include do-it-yourself work; most housework, cooking, gardening, dress-making, and knitting; and all voluntary work. All of these produce outputs which would otherwise have to be paid for and, if bought, would increase the size of GDP. Estimates of the value of unpaid housework in industrial economies are that it is about a fifth of GDP. In less developed economies, particularly those with large subsistence economies, these unpaid activities are even larger in proportion to the official output figures.

Illicit activities are a further exclusion from the official statistics. These range from the highly profitable production and distribution of illegal drugs to the plumber who prefers to be paid in cash, so as to avoid paying tax.

Another difficulty with the official figures for GDP is that they add the cost of coping with pollution to the value of ouput. For example, when a tanker runs aground and spills its cargo of crude oil, the costs of salvage of the vessel and of cleaning up the effects of the spillage are counted as an addition to GDP. As economies grow the costs of pollution tend to become larger, but they are not in any sense adding to the well-being of the country. This brings us to consider what is meant by 'the standard of living' and how it may be measured or assessed.

The **standard of living** is not a well-defined concept and it may mean different things to different people. Do the social science researcher, the district nurse, the archbishop, and the politician all mean the same when they use the term? The economist takes the national income figures as a starting point, but needs to be aware of their deficiencies. GDP is the figure most commonly used to measure a country's output and growth but national income, which is more closely linked to GNP than to GDP, is more useful when considering a country's standard of living. In practice, any of the three will be used.

There are two main kinds of difficulty with using ouput or income statistics as an indicator of living standards: these difficulties lie in omissions and in comparisons. We consider the problems of omissions from the official statistics first. The preceding section on the limitations of output figures listed the 'weightless economy', the 'underground economy', and non-market activities as contributions to output which are poorly recorded by the official statistics, or not recorded at all. Economic 'bads' such as pollution should be deductions from figures used to indicate living standards; instead they often lead to an increase in recorded output and income, as officially measured.

Output figures are unable to show how improvements in the quality of goods and services contribute to improvements in living standards: an automatic washing machine of the 1990s is far less time-consuming than an electric washing machine of the 1950s. The hours we spend in paid employment contribute to output figures, but we value our leisure time equally; no measure of the improvements in living standards associated with the gradual shortening of the working week is possible within the existing framework of output and income statistics.

The second area of difficulty lies in making comparisons, both over time and between countries, using output and income statistics. These figures express the value of output or income in terms of the current value of money, but the value of that money may change quite rapidly, sometimes even making comparisons between one year and the next meaningless. Comparisons over several decades in terms of current money are usually pointless. Such comparisons need to be made in **real terms** rather than using **nominal figures**, that is, after adjusting for any changes in the average level of prices over the time period of the comparison.

Figures of output per head, or **per capita GDP**, tell us rather more about the relative living standards of two countries than the total figures for GDP, but they do not tell us how income is distributed within a country, and so still cannot give us the full picture. Also, ways of life vary around the world – on a small tropical island there is no need for layers of warm clothing and expensive heating. Output-per-head figures may give a quite misleading impression of the comfort and pleasure of life on a tropical island, when compared to life in a northern industrial country.

Finally, national statistics are presented in terms of national currencies but the purchasing power of different currencies may not be reflected by the official exchange rates. So even if all per capita GDP figures were expressed in US dollars the results could still be misleading. In an attempt to overcome this kind of problem *The Economist* has produced its own 'Big Mac index' for several years; this index gives a guide to the purchasing power of different currencies buying a standardized product available from McDonald's around the world.

Stephen Dobson & Susan Palfreman, *Introduction to Modern Economics*, New York: Oxford University Press, 1999 (pp.161-162)

◇◇ DEFINITIONS ◇◇◇

- ♦**output** the quantity of goods and services produced in any time period in an economy
- ♦**GDP (gross domestic product)** the total money value of output produced annually by the *factors of production* (land, labor, capital, and entrepreneurship) within a country's boundaries, whoever owns them
- ♦**voluntary work** unpaid social work or charity work done by people who choose to help those in need or to do good to the public in other ways
- ♦**tax** payments made to the legal authorities to meet public expenses
- ♦**crude oil** oil produced from a reservoir after any associated gas has been removed, the raw material thus obtained is then processed at a refinery
- ♦**standard of living** a relative concept, which refers both to the monetary and non-monetary (or social) indicators which characterize a person's lifestyle; traditionally measured by a country's *gross national product* and *per capita income*
- ♦**national income** the net value of all goods and services produced annually in a nation (*GNP*) less capital consumption (i.e. depreciation); *net national product*
- ♦**growth** an increase in a country's output of goods and services over time
- ♦**GNP (gross national product)** the total money value of output produced annually by factors of production owned by the residents of a country (i.e. including payments from abroad of rent, wages, interest, dividends and profits)
- ♦**underground economy** that part of the economy in which transactions are not reported for taxation purposes, such as cash sums paid to workers and all illegal money transactions; *black economy*
- ♦**average** the arithmetic mean obtained by dividing the sum of two or more quantities by the number of items
- ♦**per capita GDP** gross domestic product of a country divided by its population; *output per head*
- ♦**currencies** the banknotes and coins in circulation in an economy used as a medium of exchange
- ♦**purchasing power** the amount of goods and services you can actually buy with your money income
- ♦**exchange rates** the prices of currencies in terms of each other

◇◇ EXERCISES ◇◇◇

◇ EXERCISE 1 *Comprehension*

True / False Circle the correct choice and justify your answer

1. 'Non-market' activities do not turn up in the official GDP figures. T / F
2. In LDCs, unpaid activities outweigh the official figures. T / F
3. Pollution costs are not recorded in GDP. T / F
4. GDP figures are the most useful point of departure for assessing living standards. T / F
5. The shortening of the working week has contributed to raising living standards. T / F

6. Currency fluctuations make all international comparisons of living standards pointless. T / F
7. Comparisons based on **real figures** do not allow for any changes in average price levels over time. T / F
8. Income distribution inside a country is the key to understanding living standards. T / F
9. Converting national currencies into US dollars enables economists to make valid international comparisons of living standards. T / F
10. The 'Big Mac index' dispenses with the need to adjust for purchasing power. T / F

◇ EXERCISE 2 *Vocabulary*

Fill in the blanks with the words listed below

expectancy / quality / real / available / measured / social / health / higher / rate / indicator / according to / equivalent / supply / developed / literacy

Measuring Development

The prime ....(1) of development remains the level of ....(2) GDP per capita, however, non-monetary or ....(3) indicators will provide us with information about the ....(4) of life in LDCs. The main indicators in this category relate to ....(5), nutrition and education. Life ....(6) at birth and the infant mortality ....(7) are much lower in less ....(8) countries than in advanced nations, whereas the adult ....(9) rate is seven times ....(10) in Australia than in Ethiopia ....(11) World Bank sources. Nutrition is ....(12) in terms of the daily calorie ....(13) per capita, which refers to the calorie ....(14) of food ....(15) to each person.

◇ EXERCISE 3 *Grammar*

Modals

Rewrite (and improve) the following sentences choosing between: *can / could / must / should / may / might*. You will need to use the **passive voice** in some cases.

Example: Statistics are sometimes misleading
Statistics *can be* misleading

1. The exchange rates were probably distorted.
2. It is necessary to raise industrial output.
3. It is quite possible that the World Bank will grant a new loan.
4. It seems very likely that the gap between rich and poor countries is widening.
5. It would have been better to foster industrial growth rather than traditional agriculture.
6. It seems uncertain that the government will adopt this policy.
7. According to the authors, economists don't pay enough attention to 'non-market' activities.

8. It is indispensable for economists to consider non-monetary indicators of living standards.
9. The government has the means of distributing economic aid more fairly.
10. It was possible for the IMF to advise this country more appropriately.

FROM THE NEWS

RICH AND POOR

European cows are better off than half the world

◇ EXERCISE

Read the article below and discuss or write answers to the following questions

1. Why would a lot of people be better off as a cow?
2. In what way is the "impact devastating"?
3. Are the UN millennium targets likely to be reached?
4. What is the point of comparing South Korea and Senegal?
5. Comment on the graph.

European cows are better off than half the world

The growing chasm between rich and poor propels migration and rewards people trafficking

For half the world's population the brutal reality is this: you'd be better off as a cow. An average European cow receives $2.20 a day from the taxpayer in subsidies and other aid. In developing countries around the world 2.8 billion people live on less than $2 a day.

The facts of global inequality are truly staggering. The richest 25 million Americans have an income equal to that of almost 2 billion people, while the assets of the world's three richest men is greater than the combined income of the world's least developed countries.

Or consider this: living standards in Sierra Leone, ranked bottom of the United Nations human development

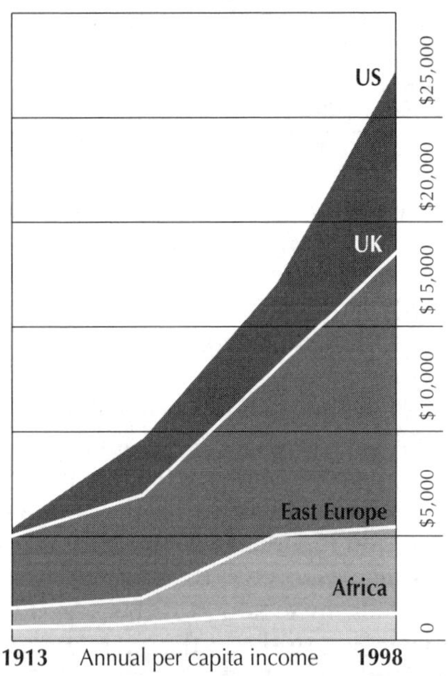

Annual per capita income

index, are roughly equivalent to those in the West 600 years ago. The average income per head stands at only $130 a year, less than the $1-a-day level that the World Bank regards as subsistence level. The impact is devastating. A Sierra Leonean can expect to live only until 37, a level not seen in the West since the industrial revolution.

Two centuries ago income per head in Britain, the world's richest country at the time, was three times higher than that of Africa, then the planet's poorest region. Today the world's richest country, Switzerland, enjoys a per capita income that is nearly 80 times higher than the world's poorest region, South Asia.

One World Bank economist has warned that, as television shows the poor the gap between their lives and the West, the rich may have to lock themselves in gated enclaves to keep out the angry masses. Grinding poverty is propelling migration, driving the best and brightest from the developing world to seek better chances elsewhere. Borders in the West are being sealed to economic migrants, with the result that people trafficking has become a more lucrative trade than drug smuggling.

Two years ago, at the UN millennium summit, world leaders set themselves the task of halving global poverty over the next 15 years. They promised to eradicate hunger, reduce under-five mortality by two-thirds and get every child of primary school age into a classroom. The cost of meeting these goals is estimated at between $40bn and $60bn on top of current aid spending – about a sixth of what the West currently spends on subsidising its farmers.

In its most recent assessment of progress, the UN said 33 countries, totalling a quarter of the world's population, are likely to miss half these targets. Most such countries are in Africa. If living standards in the poorest states rise at the current snail's pace, the UN estimates it will take 130 years to rid the world of hunger.

Extraordinary efforts will be needed to get sub-Saharan Africa back on track, the UN says. Even to halve poverty would require growth of almost 4% in income per head over the next 15 years, a heroic task for many countries where living standards are lower than they were 30 years ago.

But the task is not impossible. The proportion of the world's poor living in absolute poverty has fallen from 24% in 1990 to 20% today, because of rapid growth in east Asia.

In 1960 Senegal and South Korea had a GDP per head of $230. By 2000 South Korea had a per capital GDP of $8,910. Living standards in Senegal, however, had barely improved, with GDP per head at $260. Fifty years ago South Korea's main export was human hair; today it is a hi-tech leader supplying components for the United States' computer industry.

Africa faces a hard task following Asia's success. It is blighted by debt, conflict and unfavourable geography. South Korea was allowed to protect its infant industries, but Africa is required to open its markets by the International Monetary Fund and the World Bank. The chance of Senegal following in South Korea's footsteps seem slender as rich countries pull the development ladder up behind them. But tackling poverty is becoming a political as well as a moral imperative. A more just world would also be a more stable one.

Charlotte Denny, *Guardian Weekly*, 22 August 2002 (p.7)

CHAPTER 9

TRADE, PROTECTION AND POVERTY

◇ Key words and concepts

tariff
imports
demand
prices
domestic
competitors
output
profits
inputs
wages
bid up
alleviate
hire
labor
lured
welfare
accrue to
losses
income
trade
hence
assuming
rife
terms of trade
host
offsetting
literature
rationale
alter
outcome

Instructions For Study

1° Turn to the **definitions** following the text *Trade, Protection and Poverty*. They refer to the specialist terms printed in **bold** type in the list of **Key words and concepts.** Study them closely and pinpoint them in the text.
2° Use an **English** language dictionary to check the meanings (in context) of the other words in the list.
3° Do the exercises to test your comprehension, vocabulary and grammar skills.

Trade, Protection and Poverty

The primary effect of a tariff, and the reason for its use is that it raises domestic prices of imports and discourages demand for them. As import prices rise, domestic competitors are able to raise their prices as well, and expand their output. The increased prices lead directly to an increase in profits for the producers. At the same time, the increased output requires the use of increased inputs in production, and this is likely to cause wages and other input prices to be bid up as well. Thus, all participants in an industry that receives tariff protection are likely to benefit, in varying degrees, from increased profits and/or wages. It is through this mechanism, to the extent that any of the beneficiaries are poor, that tariffs may be able to alleviate poverty.

These positive effects are likely to be supplemented by additional benefits to individuals outside of the immediate participants in the protected industry. As output rises, the protected firms will hire more labor, either from among the unemployed or from other industries lured by offers of increased wages. Similarly, the protected industry will require additional inputs from other industries, and this secondary expansion will have similar effects in them as well.

There are, however, costs associated with protection as well as benefits. It is fundamental in the theory of international trade that tariffs tend to lower the welfare of the countries that levy them. Therefore, whatever benefits accrue to the members of the protected industry and others with whom they interact, there must also be losses elsewhere in the economy that are even greater. That is, at best, administered protection results in a transfer of income to industries, and the regions in which they operate, that make use of these trade laws and away from all other industries and regions. Hence, we treat these trade laws as policies that transfer income, rather than policies that create income. Trade theory predicts that protection will lower real national income. Therefore, by assuming that it merely transfers income we give protection the benefit of the doubt in terms of its effects on poverty.

We should also note that there are many exceptions to the rule that tariffs reduce national welfare. Trade theory is rife with these, including the terms-of-trade argument for a tariff, the infant industry argument, the national defense argument, and a host of other arguments that depend, for their effect, on the tariff offsetting some sort of domestic distortion. In addition, the recent literature on strategic trade policy has provided new rationales for trade policies as means to alter the outcome of strategic interactions among imperfectly competitive firms and their governments.

All of this literature provides the potential for tariffs to be welfare improving and could therefore improve their chances of alleviating poverty. Even those economists who have contributed the most to the literature on strategic trade policy, however, remain pessimistic about the possibility of tariffs being beneficial in the real world.

Therefore, it seems reasonable here to assume that trade actions do at best cause a transfer of income among different parts of the economy. The influence of a policy on poverty within a segment of the economy (a region or an industry) depends upon the incidence of the policy over different income groups.

Alan Deardorff & John Haveman,
The Effects of U.S. Trade Laws on Poverty in America,
The Journal of Human Resources XXX4 (Fall 1995) (pp.809, 811-812)

◇◇ DEFINITIONS ◇◇◇

- ♦**tariff** customs duties (taxes) levied (raised) by a government on imported or exported goods
- ♦**imports** goods and services bought from other countries
- ♦**demand** quantity of a good that will be bought at a given time at a given price
- ♦**prices** values expressed in terms of money
- ♦**competitors** firms which are rivals in business; *business rivals*
- ♦**output** the total quantity of goods produced
- ♦**profits** the income accruing to the entrepreneur; *earnings*
- ♦**inputs** factors of production (land, labor and capital) which are combined to make goods and services
- ♦**wages** income for labor
- ♦**hire** to take a worker on, to pay someone to do a job
- ♦**labor** human element of the production process; *workers*
- ♦**income** the return on the use of land, labor or capital; *earnings*
- ♦**trade** the activity of exchanging, or buying and selling of goods; *commerce*
- ♦**terms of trade** a measure of the trading prospects of a country (favourable or unfavourable) in terms of the prices of its imports in relation to the prices of its exports
- ♦**rationale** the fundamental reason which serves as the basis or justification for a policy

◇◇ EXERCISES ◇◇◇

◇ EXERCISE 1 *Comprehension*

True / False Circle the correct choice and justify your answer

1. Tariffs are implemented to aid the domestic economy. T / F
2. There are seldom spin-offs outside the protected industry. T / F
3. It is essential to carry out a cost-benefit analysis of tariff protection. T / F
4. We can be sure that tariff protection will alleviate poverty. T / F
5. It is difficult to find arguments for tariffs promoting national welfare. T / F

◇ EXERCISE 2 *Vocabulary*

Find sentences in the text which refer to the following

1. Salaries will probably be increased.
2. Tariffs can help to raise the standard of living.
3. Companies will take on more workers.
4. Jobless workers and those from other industries will be attracted to higher wages.

5. Tariffs have a tendency to undermine the well-being of countries that impose them.
6. Studies on strategic trade policy have opened the way for a fresh approach to the matter.
7. The latest writings tend to come down on the side of tariffs.
8. Many arguments are based on the assumption that tariffs will compensate for internal imbalances.

◇ EXERCISE 3 *Grammar*

Tenses

Complete the sentences below choosing between the **simple past** or the **present perfect** tense

1. The effects of tariffs (always / to be) difficult to assess accurately.
2. Some domestic producers (to become) very rich during the boom years.
3. The WTO (to set up) new trade rules over recent years.
4. Indonesia (to have) a per capita GDP of $664 in 2000 compared to $23,760 in France.
5. The World Bank (generally / to back) labour-intensive activities in developing countries.
6. The recent literature on trade policy (to provide) governments with new economic strategies.
7. The protected firms (to hire) more labour when their output rose.
8. Tariffs (usually / to tend to) lower the welfare of countries that implement them.

FROM THE BUSINESS NEWS

DUMPING

Subsidies sweeten EU sugar exports

◇ EXERCISE

Read the article below and discuss or write answers to the following questions

1. Who is financing Europe's sugar industry profits?
2. How does the deal work?
3. Is there something "insane" about this situation?
4. How are the cheaper producers kept out of Europe?
5. Who are the losers?

Subsidies sweeten EU sugar exports

Europe's sugar industry is receiving a £1bn handout from taxpayers and consumers, allowing it to dump millions of tonnes of subsidised sugar on international markets at the expense of some of the world's poorest farmers, a report claimed last week.

British Sugar, a Peterborough-based processing firm, is one of a handful of companies making huge profits under a price-fixing deal set by Brussels that pays farmers and firms up to three times the going world rate for their sugar.

The deal has enabled sugar beet farmers in Germany, Britain and France to become the world's largest exporters of white sugar despite being the world's most expensive producers, according to Oxfam. African countries such as Mozambique and Senegal are the biggest losers.

"In a sane world Europe would be importing its sugar," said Kate Raworth, policy researcher Oxfam and the report's author. "Instead, European consumers and taxpayers are paying to destroy livelihoods in some of the world's poorest countries."

It costs €670 (£430) to produce a tonne of white sugar in Europe compared with just €280 in countries such as Brazil, Ethiopia, Senegal and Mozambique. Duties of up to 140% on foreign imports shut most low-cost producers out of Europe.

The biggest winners are the sugar processors such as British Sugar, many of which are effectively government monopolies with a licence from Brussels to charge consumers excessive prices, according to Ms Raworth. British Sugar, which controls the entire British sugar beet quota, made profits in excess of 20% last year, according to Oxfam, at a time when most of the food industry was struggling.

The firms allocate the quotas to farmers, buy the sugar at a price fixed by the EU, process it and then sell it to retailers at a guaranteed minimum price. Oxfam estimates that if prices were lowered so British Sugar made returns more in line with industries where there is competition, British consumers would save £77m a year.

British Sugar said its profitability came from "efficient operation of our businesses."

Oxfam says guaranteed prices encourage overproduction. The resulting sugar mountain is dumped on world markets at a heavily subsidised rate, depressing international prices.

Charlotte Denny, *Guardian Weekly*, 29 August 2002 (p.8)

PART D

LABOR ECONOMICS

IN THIS PART YOU WILL READ ABOUT

- Industrial relations in Britain
- A labor dispute in the Fire Brigade
- Unemployment: stock and flow concepts
- The working population and labor force
- EU aid to small and medium-sized enterprises
- The efficiency of labor
- Immigrants in American society

YOU WILL LEARN SOME BASIC ECONOMIC TERMS CONCERNING

- Trade unions
- Unemployment benefits
- Claimants and job seekers
- The underground economy
- Disadvantaged workers
- Union contracts

CHAPTER 10

TRADE UNIONS IN BRITAIN

◇ Key words and concepts

trade unions
Labour Party
working conditions
membership
unemployment
regulatory legislation
Conservative government
skilled workers
Law Society
white-collar workers
range
businesses
subscriptions
elect
latter
support
strike pay
official strikes
political spectrum
trade
comprise
public service
scheme
victimization
Trades Union Congress
conference
currently
recession
union officials
enforce
pickets
premises
secondary action
fined
wage demands
pay claims
workplaces

Instructions For Study

1° Turn to the **definitions** following the text *Trade Unions in Britain*. They refer to the specialist terms printed in **bold** type in the list of **Key words and concepts.** Study them closely and pinpoint them in the text.
2° Use an **English** language dictionary to check the meanings (in context) of the other words in the list.
3° Do the exercises to test your comprehension, vocabulary and grammar skills.

Trade Unions in Britain

The modern trade unions are associated with the Labour Party, and campaign for better working, health and pay conditions for their members. The trade-union movement is highly organized and has a membership of 8.3 million people, though this marks a fall from over 12 million in 1978. The reduction has been due to rises in unemployment; changing attitudes to trade unions among workers; industrial decline; and regulatory legislation by Conservative governments.

Today there are some 350 trade unions and professional associations of workers, which vary considerably in size and influence. They represent not only skilled and unskilled workers in industry, but also white-collar workers in a range of businesses, companies and local and central government. Other professional associations like the Law Society, the Police Federation and the British Medical Association carry out similar representational roles for their members.

Members of trade unions pay annual subscriptions to their unions and frequently to the Labour Party, unless they elect not to pay this latter amount. This funding provides for union activities and services, such as legal, monetary and professional help. The richer unions are able to give strike pay to members who are taking part in 'official strikes', which are those legally sanctioned by members. Trade unions vary in their wealth and in their political orientation, ranging from the far left to the right wing of the political spectrum.

Some unions admit as members only those people who work in a specific trade or profession, such as miners or teachers. Other unions comprise workers who are employed in different or more general areas of industry or commerce, like the Transport and General Workers' Union. Smaller unions have frequently joined with others in similar fields to form new unions, such as Unison, which comprises public service workers and which is now the largest in Britain with 1.4 million members. Workers may choose, without victimization, whether they want to belong to a particular union or none at all.

Many trade unions are affiliated to the Trades Union Congress (TUC), which was founded in 1868 and serves as an umbrella organization to coordinate trade union interests. It holds an annual conference and can be successful in promoting cooperation among workers. In the past, it exerted some political pressure on government, usually when Labour has been in power. It is currently seeking to extend its contacts in industry and commerce and with employers as well as workers.

The influence of the TUC and trade unions has, however, declined, due to the effects of unemployment, the restructuring of industry after recession, and Conservative legislation. Laws were passed to enforce secret voting by union members before strikes can be legally called and for the election of union officials. The number of pickets (union strikers) outside business premises has been reduced, secondary (or sympathy) action by other unionists is banned, and unions may be fined by the courts if they transgress legislation. Such laws (which the Labour government accept) and the economic climate forced trade unions to be more realistic in their wage demands in the 1980s. But pay claims are now escalating again, and there is also pressure for the legal recognition of unions in those workplaces where a majority of workers want them.

John Oakland, *British Civilisation*, London: Routledge, 2000 (pp.206-209)

◇◇ DEFINITIONS ◇◇◇

♦ **trade unions** workers' organizations set up to defend the rights and interests of their members
♦ **Labour Party** left-of-centre political party, supported by the trade unions, the working class and part of the middle-class
♦ **working conditions** factors affecting the work environment, such as hours of work, safety arrangements, fringe benefits
♦ **unemployment** the situation of being jobless when willing and able to work
♦ **regulatory legislation** laws introduced to limit or control (regulate) the way an organization is run
♦ **Conservative government** right-of-centre government in power from 1979 to 1997, supported mainly by business interests and the middle and upper classes
♦ **skilled workers** those who have acquired, through training or apprenticeship, the special abilities required to do certain work
♦ **white-collar workers** office workers, clerical staff, managerial and professional people
♦ **Law Society** the solicitors' trade union as well as their governing body
♦ **businesses** firms, trading establishments, commercial organizations
♦ **subscriptions** the contributions that a union member pays regularly to his organization; *dues*
♦ **strike pay** an allowance paid out of union funds to members on strike
♦ **official strikes** those that take place in accordance with union instructions
♦ **trade** a manual occupation requiring a special skill
♦ **public service** sector of a nation's economy covering government and local authority activities
♦ **Trades Union Congress (TUC)** central trade union confederation to which most British trade unions belong
♦ **recession** a slowdown in economic activity; *slump*
♦ **union officials** elected or appointed officers of trade unions who represent members and organize union business
♦ **pickets** striking workers stationed at factory gates to persuade others not to enter the premises
♦ **secondary action** when a trade union calls out its workers in support of industrial action by unionists elsewhere; *sympathy action*
♦ **wage demands** union requests for improved pay; *pay claims*
♦ **pay claims** union demands for better wages; *wage demands*

◇◇ EXERCISES ◇◇◇

◇ EXERCISE 1 ***Comprehension***

True / False Circle the correct choice and justify your answer

1. Regulatory legislation by the Conservatives halted the decline in union numbers. T / F

2. Unions give financial backing systematically to their members on strike. T / F
3. The current economic climate has put pressure on workers to tone down wage demands. T / F
4. The TUC is primarily involved in the organizing of blue-collar workers. T / F
5. Picketing outside plants which are not involved in a dispute is prohibited. T / F

◇ EXERCISE 2 *Vocabulary*

Use the list of definitions above to **select the appropriate term** to fit each sentence

1. Trade guilds and social clubs were originally set up to protect their members against sickness and ....
2. Most manufacturing plants and .... are free of strikes.
3. The strikers said they would not go back to work until their .... were met.
4. .... leadership in Britain has undoubtedly become more left-wing and militant in recent years.
5. The new leader of Amicus (the engineering and electricians' union), Derek Simpson, says he is opposed to such iconic leftist action as ....
6. The unions will have to ballot their members in 2003 on whether to maintain a political fund, used to finance the ....
7. Thousands of workers have been laid off in manufacturing owing to the ....
8. .... were stationed outside the premises to prevent any coal deliveries.
9. Many industrial disputes are over pay and ....
10. Unison mainly represents .... workers.

◇ EXERCISE 3 *Grammar*

(A) How long, since, for or ago?

Make sentences using the correct expression

1. this trade union / industrial action / December / involved
2. that strike / going on
3. several years / compulsory / secret ballots / been
4. outside the premises / pickets / stationed
5. TUC / that labor union / 1984 / affiliated to

(B) Tenses

Circle the alternative (a), (b), (c) or (d) that corresponds to the **correct form of the verb**

1. The strikers are anxious to see how much support they .... from the public.
   a) obtained
   b) have obtained
   c) will obtain
   d) could have obtained

2. Other companies .... to take similar industrial action.
   a) expected
   b) are expected

c) could expect
d) have expected

3. The manager hoped the workers on the shop floor .... their shop stewards.
   a) will ignore
   b) would have ignored
   c) ignore
   d) would ignore

4. The union spokesman said that the strikers .... the law.
   a) were not breaking
   b) have broken
   c) breaking
   d) should break

5. The Employment Secretary said that all the parties involved in the dispute ....
   a) negotiating
   b) should negotiate
   c) have negotiated
   d) will not negotiate

FROM THE INDUSTRIAL FRONT

LABOR UNREST

Blair gets tough with firemen

◇ EXERCISE

Read the article below and discuss or write answers to the following questions

1. What sort of a bargain is Tony Blair going for?
2. Can Tony Blair be said to be trying to get political mileage out of the dispute?
3. Why are the strikers so angry?
4. What industrial action does the union have in mind?
5. What are the Tories doing?

Blair gets tough with firemen

THE PRIME Minister stepped into the firemen's dispute on Monday as the strikers started their fourth day on picket lines around the country.

After a weekend of bitter recriminations following the collapse of peace talks in the early hours of Friday morning, Tony Blair brought forward his monthly press conference to warn the Fire Brigades Union it could not win the dispute and to praise troops who are providing emergency cover.

Mr Blair told a Downing Street briefing that no extra money would be given to settle the row unless it was paid for through changes in working practices. The firemen are seeking a 40 per cent pay rise.

Union and council negotiators have accused John Prescott, the Deputy Prime Minister, of intervening to wreck a peace deal worked out in the early hours before the strike.

The two sides had been close to an agreement on a 16 per cent deal but Mr Blair said that had not been costed and would have required more money from the Government.

Mr Blair attacked the union for what he called its "unreasonable" pay demand, claiming that victory for them "would not be a defeat for the Government, it would be a defeat for the country."

Firemen were swift to respond to the Prime Minister's speech. Even before Mr Blair had finished strikers at Glasgow's Govan fire station were working on a sign which read "Lying Blairstard."

The strikers raised their voices in anger above the cacophony of car horns sounded in support by passing drivers and vowed to fight on. Chris McGlone, 38, a station officer with 15 years' experience, said: "The Government have obviously taken a decision that they will have us out for as long as possible. This is Blair throwing down the gauntlet to all public sector workers."

Gordon Wilson, 45, who has 20 years' experience, said: "Blair, Brown and Prescott seem to forget that they are public sector workers too. They awarded themselves a 40 per cent pay rise and we want the same."

The union has called for two more eight-day-long strikes, starting on December 4 and 16, unless there is a breakthrough in their deadlocked dispute.

Ian Duncan Smith called Mr Blair's decision to call in TV cameras rather than make a Commons statement an "outrageous abuse of Parliament."

The Tory leader said: "This is not the time for engineering stage-managed media opportunities in Downing Street. The Government has completely lost the plot."

Benedict Brogan & Alan Jones,
Daily Telegraph Weekly, 27 November 2002 (p.1)

CHAPTER 11

MEASURING UNEMPLOYMENT

◇ Key words and concepts

achievement
unemployment rate
RPI
labour force
claimant count
Job Seeker's Allowance
retirement age
work-related schemes
inconsistency
quoted
working population
unemployment benefits
recorded
underemployment
computation
available
quarterly
overnight
underground economy
added to
altered
average
life expectancy
natural rate of unemployment
retraining

Instructions For Study

1° Turn to the **definitions** following the text *Measuring Unemployment*. They refer to the specialist terms printed in **bold** type in the list of **Key words and concepts.** Study them closely and pinpoint them in the text.
2° Use an **English** language dictionary to check the meanings (in context) of the other words in the list.
3° Do the exercises to test your comprehension, vocabulary and grammar skills.

Measuring Unemployment

Achievement of the third macroeconomic goal of full employment is measured by the **unemployment rate**, which, with the RPI, is one of the most politically sensitive economic indicators. Internationally, the unemployment rate is understood to show the number of people without a job and looking for work as a percentage of the **labour force**.

In practice this is not easy to measure and depends very much on definitions of what is meant by 'without work', 'looking for work', and 'the labour force'. You might think these definitions are obvious but, partly because of the politically sensitive nature of the resulting figures, definitions have been changed several times in the UK in the last twenty years. This makes comparisons over any period of time difficult and has led to a widespread and unfortunate cynicism about the validity of government statistics in general. Until April 1998, the UK unemployment figures were based on a **claimant count**: they showed the numbers of adult workers not employed and claiming the Job Seeker's Allowance. Therefore the unemployment figures excluded those under 18 and those over 60 years of age, even though the retirement age for men is 65, while the UK employment figures showed the number of workers over 16 with a job and those on government work-related schemes – an obvious inconsistency.

Changes in the bases on which the unemployment data were collected in recent years have generally had the effect of reducing the quoted unemployment rate. In particular, the unemployed have been shown as a percentage of the working population rather than of the labour force. The working population is larger than the labour force because it includes the armed forces and the self-employed; therefore the unemployment rate looks lower than it might, had the previous definition been still in use.

There are several other ways in which the published unemployment statistics underestimate unemployment as the term is understood by most people. Women who stop working to raise a family and then wish to return to work may not claim unemployment benefits and so are excluded from the recorded unemployment figures, as are school leavers and men between the ages of 60 and 65. People who are unemployed for only a brief period are also excluded. There is no way of indicating the extent of underemployment either, whether of the part-time employee who would prefer full-time work, or of the over-qualified employee such as a biologist with a Ph.D. who works in McDonald's serving hamburgers.

However, from April 1998, the published UK unemployment rate has conformed to international standards of computation and has been based on a monthly estimate of the number of people seeking jobs and available to work, derived from the quarterly Labour Force Survey. This change added about half a million people to the jobless total, overnight.

On the other hand government figures may also overestimate unemployment. Some claims for unemployment benefits are fraudulent because those claiming have an undeclared income from employment in the underground economy; similarly some people with seasonal work may prefer not to work all year round but may sign on the unemployment register when not employed.

Stocks and flows

Unemployment is a **stock**, measured at one point in time, while people becoming unemployed or finding a job are a **flow**, measured over a period of time. Stock and flow concepts are central to macroeconomics – they are, for example, relevant to the circular-flow model. The figure below shows how the pool of unemployed people is added to by those who lose their jobs or who return to or join the labour force; it is reduced by those who leave the labour force by retiring, emigrating, dying, caring for children or relatives, or giving up the search, and by those who get a job. If the flows into the pool are greater than the flows out then the level of the pool will rise, that is, the stock or the number unemployed becomes larger and the unemployment rate rises. In any one year the flows in and out of the pool are significantly greater than the number unemployed at any one moment.

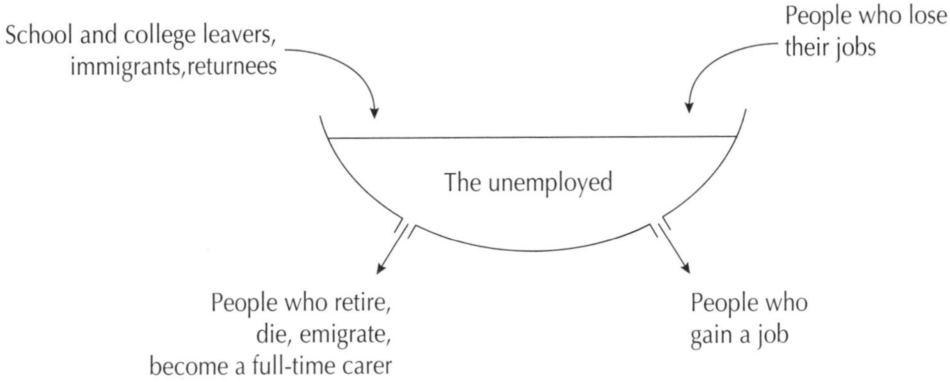

Changes in unemployment: stock and flow concepts

The size of the labour force is greater than the size of the employed population but smaller than the population of official working age. Over the years changes in society have meant that the composition of the labour force has altered and changes in the economy have meant that the sort of work offered by employers has also altered. In the last fifty years an increasing proportion of women has entered the labour force; the school-leaving age has risen and a higher proportion of school leavers go on into further or higher education, thus entering the labour force several years later; and the average retirement age has fallen but average life expectancy has risen. During the same period there has been a decline in employment in heavy industry and a rise in employment in the service sector; there has been a decline in employment in manual labour and a rise in employment in high-technology industries; and there has been a significant growth in the numbers of those in part-time employment. All these factors may combine to affect the natural rate of unemployment, since much of the labour force is relatively immobile geographically and retraining is not universally available or acceptable.

Stephen Dobson & Susan Palfreman, *Introduction to Modern Economics*, New York: Oxford University Press, 1999 (pp.168-170)

◇◇ DEFINITIONS ◇◇◇

◆ **unemployment rate** a measure of the number of jobless people, willing and able to work, expressed as a percentage of the labour force

◆ **RPI (Retail Prices Index)** a measure of the cost of living, i.e. of changes in the prices of goods in shops (retail prices) and changes in the price of services bought by households

◆ **labour force** adults in employment or looking for a job

◆ **claimant count** the numbers of adult workers not employed and applying for unemployment benefits

◆ **Job Seeker's Allowance** unemployment benefit paid to jobless people to provide them with some minimum standard of living until they can find a new paid job

◆ **retirement age** the age at which someone withdraws permanently from regular or active employment

◆ **work-related schemes** a government-run programme whereby unemployed people are provided with some form of temporary or part-time employment (e.g. welfare to work which encourages people on welfare to join the workforce)

◆ **working population** adults in employment or looking for a job plus the armed forces and the self-employed

◆ **unemployment benefits** transfer payments in cash or kind made to jobless people; *unemployment compensation*

◆ **underemployment** the condition that exists when someone works at a job which does not fully utilize their capacity or ability

◆ **underground economy** that part of the economy in which transactions are not reported for taxation purposes, such as cash sums paid to workers and all illegal money transactions; *black economy*

◆ **average** the arithmetic mean obtained by dividing the sum of two or more quantities by the number of items

◆ **life expectancy** the average age to which a category of persons will live

◆ **natural rate of unemployment** is the unemployment rate at full employment, or when the labour market is in equilibrium; it includes frictional and structural unemployment

◆ **retraining** teaching workers to acquire new skills

◇◇ EXERCISES ◇◇◇

◇ EXERCISE 1 *Comprehension*

Circle the alternative (a), (b) or (c) that most fully and correctly completes the statements below

1. It is not easy to measure unemployment
   (a) because government statistical methods are not valid
   (b) because defining key terms and expressions is not an easy task
   (c) because of the difficulty of collecting data

2. Changes in the computation of unemployment rates over the years have tended to
   (a) inflate unemployment figures
   (b) overestimate the claimant count
   (c) underestimate the real figures

3. Some fraudulent claims for unemployment benefits are due to
   (a) people who work in the black economy
   (b) seasonal workers
   (c) ill-kept unemployment registers

4. The size of the labour force is greater than the size of the employed population
   (a) insofar as the armed forces do not belong to the working population
   (b) insofar as the self-employed are extremely numerous
   (c) insofar as many employable adults are out of work

5. Over the last fifty years there has been
   (a) a decline in the use of both manual labour and of knowledge workers
   (b) a rise in employment in the services, in high-tech and in part-time activities
   (c) a decline in heavy industry and retraining schemes

◇ EXERCISE 2 *Vocabulary*

Use the list of definitions above to **select the appropriate term** to fit each sentence

1. An example of .... is when an economics professor is working as a clerk.
2. The spending pattern of the average household enables the .... to be computed.
3. The .... measure in use in Britain over recent years has been replaced by the international definition.
4. The stock and flow concepts are central to understanding trends in the ....
5. Frictional and structural unemployment are an integral part of the ....
6. The rise in the average .... constitutes one of several factors affecting the size of the labour force in Britain.
7. The government set up a benefit fraud hotline in 1999 to help detect dishonest .... claims.
8. The purchase and sale of alcohol in the US prohibition era of the 1920s is an example of the ....
9. Providing .... for laid-off workers is one way of improving their employability.
10. The majority of wage-earners exit the labour market when they reach ....

◇ EXERCISE 3 *Grammar*

Have something **done** *Versus* **have** someone **do** something

(A) Make sentences using the structure **have** something **done.** Pay attention to the correct tense of the verb.

1. Claimants / unemployment benefits / **process** / by a government employee
2. Wage-earners / pay / **adjust** / cost of living / generally
3. The government / last week / RPI / again / **check**
4. He / Job Seeker's Allowance / next week / new claim / **examine**
5. They / hotline / recently / to curtail / **set up** / benefit fraud

(B) Re-write the following sentences using the structure **have** someone **do** something

1. Someone is going to cancel his benefits.
   He ....
2. Someone repairs their car in a back-street garage.
   They ....
3. Someone is revising those unemployment figures for the government.
   The government ....
4. Someone should set up retraining schemes for those job seekers.
   You ....
5. Someone has excluded school leavers from the recorded unemployment figures.
   We ....

FROM THE BUSINESS NEWS

GETTING EUROPE TO WORK

EU to ease aid on jobs for disadvantaged

◇ EXERCISE

Read the article below and discuss or write answers to the following questions

1. What is the philosophy behind the European Commission's plans?
2. Will the Commission have to vet this state aid to companies?
3. Who would qualify for these jobs?
4. Will SMEs benefit from the new guidelines?
5. What do you think personally of these measures?

EU to ease aid on jobs for disadvantaged

European Union companies will be free to receive state aid to hire disadvantaged workers, such as the young unemployed and former convicts, under plans to be presented by the European Commission next week.

The Brussels authorities believe the measures could help Europe to fight unemployment by encouraging companies to employ workers from less privileged backgrounds.

Mario Monti, European competition commissioner, is a sworn enemy of state aid but is known to be in favour of targeted subsidies to alleviate problems such as unemployment.

"Our aim is that state aid should help those firms and those categories of workers that face particular difficulties," a Commission official said yesterday.

Under the plans, companies will not have to seek approval from European competition regulators for government subsidies used to hire disadvantaged workers.

At present, the European Commission has to vet this kind of state aid, which is usually given in the form of tax breaks or reduced social security contributions.

Although Brussels usually authorises these subsidies, the process can be costly and time-consuming, deterring some companies from applying for the aid.

The new rules, which are expected to be approved by the 20 commissioners on Wednesday, exempt from Brussels scrutiny state aid used to employ nine categories of disadvantaged workers, such as young people under 25 at their first job and legal immigrants.

Ethnic minority workers, the long-term unemployed, people over 55 with no job, and anyone who has been unemployed for more than a year would also qualify.

The rules, which replace existing guidelines, also include socially disadvantaged people such as former convicts, former drug addicts and women who live in areas where female unemployment is higher than the male average.

Under the rules, small and medium-sized enterprises will be allowed to receive up to twice the amount of aid as larger companies.

SMEs will be able to receive in state aid up to 15 per cent of the overall cost of a project such as a new factory, to provide jobs for disadvantaged workers. For larger firms, the threshold will be 7.5 per cent of the overall value of the project.

The proposals are set to be welcomed by several member states, such as Italy, Spain, Portugal and Greece, where youth and female unemployment is a serious problem.

Francesco Guerrera, *Financial Times*,
25 October 2002 (p.17)

CHAPTER 12

THE SUPPLY OF LABOUR AND THE QUALITY OF LABOUR

◇ Key words and concepts

supply
labour
commonly
effectiveness
offset
productivity
secured
moonlighting
available
skilled labour
craft
trained
lawyers
accountants
operatives
range
assembly plant
word-processing
on the job (training)
used to
tiring
withstand
wasting
servicing
assemblies
labour force
knowledgeable
diet
welfare services
standard of living
pace
incentives
backed
power
wealth
supported by
array

◇ Vocabulary aid

spot-welder	soudeur par points
stator winder	enrouleur de stator
ploughboy	laboureur
navvy	terrassier
cane-worker	ouvrier dans les plantations de canne à sucre
drilling	perçage

Instructions For Study

1° Turn to the **definitions** following the text *The Supply of Labour and the Quality of Labour*. They refer to the specialist terms printed in **bold** type in the list of **Key words and concepts.** Study them closely and pinpoint them in the text.
2° Use an **English** language dictionary to check the meanings (in context) of the other words in the list.
3° Do the exercises to test your comprehension, vocabulary and grammar skills.

The Supply of Labour and the Quality of Labour

If the working week is reduced the supply of labour falls, unless the resultant improvement in health enables more efficient labour to take place in the shorter working week. For instance, in early industrial Britain men, women and children commonly worked a 12-14-hour day. It is probable that the Ten Hour Act, introduced in 1847 to reduce the working day, improved the effectiveness of the work done in the ten hours to offset the shorter day. This is probably not true of present-day conditions, where, for example, reducing the 40-hour week to 35 hours almost certainly lowers the supply of labour. Productivity may still rise if the reduction of hours is secured by the workers in return for an agreement to use new machinery, etc., but the factor capital has produced the increase. Holiday periods operate in a similar way to reduce the supply of labour. An extreme example is the case of the Californian shipyard which is currently giving its workers 91 days' holiday a year. In the US generally a 30-hour week is quite common. Some workers prefer extra income to shorter working hours, so that 'moonlighting' (doing one job by day and another in the evening) is quite common. 'Moonlighting' therefore increases the supply of labour available to entrepreneurs.

More important perhaps than the actual supply of labour is the quality of the labour. Is it skilled, semi-skilled or unskilled? Is it willing? Is it adaptable? Skilled labour is labour which has either mastered a particular craft, like toolmaking or printing, or has been professionally trained, like doctors, dentists, lawyers and accountants. Semi-skilled labour is in some ways a misnomer, since the operatives who are described as semi-skilled have in fact reached very high degrees of skill over a very limited range of activities. A spot-welder in a motor-vehicle assembly plant and a stator winder in a vacuum-cleaner factory are examples. Such labour can be very quickly trained, in from four to six weeks at the most. Similarly, one manufacturer of word-processing machines considers that an operator can be fully trained in two days. Unskilled labour, as its name implies, requires little specialised training. What training there is can be acquired on the job itself. Even so this labour becomes more efficient as it grows used to the work. When the canals were dug in Britain, and later when railways were laid, the entrepreneurs found it took a full year to turn a strong, healthy ploughboy into a navvy. Not only did he need to learn the economy of effort which would enable him to work long hours without tiring but his whole physique had to change. To build the muscles that were necessary for the work, and to acquire the strength of character to withstand the rough life was not the work of a single day.

Generally speaking, skilled labour tends to be more *specific* than semi-skilled or unskilled labour. The idea of 'specificity' is an important one in economics. If a factor of production is specific it can be used in only one particular task: for instance, a dentist must be employed in dentistry if his true talents are to be used. If we take a dentist and turn him into the fields to cut sugar cane we shall be wasting his talents. Of course it may do the dentist a world of good to find out what a hard life the cane-worker leads, but this is no substitute for the efficient use of his services in caring for his patients' teeth. A spot-welder in a motor-car factory is a less specific form of labour. He will probably be equally useful servicing cars in a garage, or drilling assemblies in an electronics factory.

Factors affecting the efficiency of labour include:

(*a*) The general education and background knowledge of the labour force. If it has been born into the television era of an advanced society it will be knowledgeable, adaptable and sophisticated. If it has only recently left a peasant community it will be unsophisticated, superstitious, nervous and slow to adapt itself.

(*b*) The general health of the labour force. This may be improved by diet, and by adequate welfare services of all sorts. A developing nation's progress may be slow because a fully effective labour force depends on raising the standard of living. This is a slow process and depends on an efficient labour force. We therefore have a vicious circle, which spirals slowly upwards, but at an increasing pace as the years go by.

(*c*) The incentives offered to labour. Where there are few incentives labour will be less efficient. Where the incentives are great labour will apply itself more assiduously.

(*d*) The availability of other factors of high quality. This is the commonest method of increasing the efficiency of labour. If it is backed by good quality land, labour itself will be more efficient. If it is backed by well chosen tools and adequate power supplies, even a poor labour force will be highly productive. One explanation of the great wealth of the US is that during his or her working hours every worker is supported by an array of power tools appropriate to his or her activities.

Geoffrey Whitehead, *Economics*, Oxford: Butterworth-Heinemann, 1996 (pp.27-28)

◇◇ DEFINITIONS ◇◇◇

♦**supply** quantity of a commodity available on the market at a given time
♦**labour** human element of the production process; *workers*
♦**productivity** the relation between the amount produced (output) and one unit of land, labour or capital used (input) to produce that output
♦**moonlighting** doing one job by day and another in the evening, working illegally
♦**skilled labour** working people who have acquired expertise or know-how enabling them to perform a task efficiently
♦**craft** an activity or job that involves making or doing things skilfully
♦**trained** taught to use a particular skill or special knowledge to do a job
♦**lawyers** someone who has studied law and is legally authorized to represent people in court or in other circumstances
♦**accountants** people whose job it is to keep a record of the financial transactions (the accounts) of a business or other organization
♦**operatives** workers employed in a factory, usually operating (controlling and using) a machine or apparatus; *operators*
♦**assembly plant** factory in which a conveyor belt carries the work under construction between lines of employees, each of whom performs a given operation or makes only one part of a product
♦**word-processing** a method of creating and editing text on a computer
♦**on the job (training)** training which takes place at the workplace and in which an employee is placed in a job and trained to perform tasks under close supervision
♦**assemblies** two or more subassemblies joined together to form a complete item; a *subassembly* is a unit assembled separately but designed to be incorporated with other such units into a larger manufactured product
♦**labour force** adults in employment or looking for a job; *workforce*
♦**welfare services** government provision of health, education, housing and social security
♦**standard of living** a relative concept, which refers both to the monetary and non-monetary (or social) indicators which characterize a person's lifestyle; traditionally measured by a country's *gross national product* and *per capita income*
♦**incentives** something that gives an employee a desire to work harder, such as the payment of a bonus if his output is greater than an agreed amount

◇◇ EXERCISES ◇◇◇

◇ EXERCISE 1 *Comprehension*

Answer these questions

1. Can the introduction of the Ten Hour Act in 1847 be compared to the bringing-in of the 35-hour week today?
2. What is the difference between training semi-skilled workers in a factory today, and training a labourer in Britain in the nineteenth century?
3. What is the difference between skilled labour and semi-skilled labour? Give examples.

4. What is one factor holding back developing countries?
5. What is a determining factor in making a labour force productive?

◇ EXERCISE 2 *Vocabulary*

Use the list of definitions above to **select the appropriate term** to fit each sentence

1. .... has revolutionized the way in which an operator can be trained.
2. .... are one of many schemes devised to encourage productivity in industry.
3. .... has traditionally been defined as a measure of affluence.
4. Insufficient .... has often been linked to poor productivity.
5. The underground economy provides a convenient opportunity for ....
6. .... are trained not to deviate from job specifications.
7. Automobile manufacturing is traditionally based on .... production.
8. Improvements in .... depend very much on raising the efficiency of labour.
9. There is no substitute for .... in raising developing nations' productivity.
10. The labour force has to be .... adequately if its efficiency is to increase.

◇ EXERCISE 3 *Grammar*

For, since or ago?

Fill in the blanks using the correct expression

1. Many years ...., the general health of the labour force was poor.
2. Semi-skilled workers have been using computers .... a number of years.
3. The general education of workers has risen substantially .... the late nineteenth century.
4. .... these figures were published, new data has been collected.
5. The 35-hour week has been in force .... a year.
6. Jobless numbers have remained stable .... December count.
7. Word-processing machines were introduced into factories over a decade ....
8. He has been moonlighting .... he left school.
9. These tools were invented long ....
10. Welfare services have been curtailed .... the end of last year.

FROM THE BUSINESS NEWS

THE US WORKFORCE

Immigrants account for half of new workers

◇ EXERCISE

Read the article below and discuss or write answers to the following questions

1. What role did immigrants play in the US economy over the past decade?
2. Were new immigrants able to halt the decline in the Washington workforce?

3. What has been the impact of new immigrants on the US workforce over recent years?
4. Do immigrants hurt American-born workers?
5. Can any comparisons be drawn with trends in the diversity of the European labor force over the same period?

Immigrants account for half of new workers

A new study of census data concludes that recent immigrants were critical to the nation's economic growth in the past decade, accounting for half of the new wage earners who joined the labor force in those years.

The effect was particularly large among men: Eight of 10 new male workers in the decade were immigrants who arrived during that time, according to the report by the Center for Labor Market Studies at North-eastern University. New immigrants accounted for 76 percent of the labor force growth in Maryland and 44 percent in Virginia. In Washington, where the workforce declined, immigrants prevented further shrinkage.

The report offers powerful new evidence of the growing impact of immigrants in American society. Earlier data from the 2000 Census showed a record number of new arrivals during the 1990s that prevented population loss in some cities and rural areas. The newly analyzed workforce numbers show that immigration also is redrawing the profile of the U.S. workforce, in some cases transforming entire industries.

More than 13 million immigrants came to the United States from 1990 to 2001 – legally or illegally – drawn by the healthy economy and family ties. The report said 8 million joined the labor force, which means they were working or looking for work over a period when the total number of new workers was 16 million.

The impact on the workforce was significantly larger than in previous decades. In the 1970s, for example, immigrants accounted for 10 percent of the labor force growth. It increased to roughly a quarter in the '80s before expanding to half in the '90s. Even so, 86 percent of the workforce is American-born.

For decades, immigration policy has been a subject of intense debate, with critics saying the large numbers strain schools and other government services and take jobs from American-born workers. One of the authors of the Northeastern study argues that the research indicates the opposite: The U.S. economy would have stumbled in the past decade without the new arrivals, and most immigrants contribute more in taxes than they use in services.

"The American economy absolutely needs immigrants", said Andrew Sum, director of the labor market center. "I realize some workers have been hurt by this, and some people get very angry when I say this, but our economy has become more dependent on immigrant labor than at any time in the last 100 years."

PART E

MANAGEMENT

IN THIS PART YOU WILL READ ABOUT

- Setting up a company
- The workings of stock markets
- Job roles in large organisations
- Strategic alliances in the European Union
- Management methods in large organisations
- Direct marketing
- The Marketing Mix
- Inventory control systems
- Customer account management

YOU WILL LEARN SOME BASIC MANAGEMENT TERMS CONCERNING

- Company types and structure
- Job positions
- Globalisation
- Marketing
- Stock management
- Credit management

CHAPTER 13

COMPANIES

◇ Key words and concepts

company
shareholder
promoter
registrar of companies
authorised capital
issued capital
a call
paid up capital
private companies
family businesses
stock exchange
board of directors
unlimited liability businesses
limited liability businesses
public company
quotation on the stock exchange
takeover bid
stock exchange council
placing
underwrite shares
rights issue

Instructions For Study

1° Turn to the **definitions** following the text *Companies*. They refer to the specialist terms printed in **bold** type in the list of **Key words and concepts**. Study them closely and pinpoint them in the text.
2° Use an **English** language dictionary to check the meanings (in context) of the other words in the list.
3° Do the exercises to test your comprehension, vocabulary and grammar skills.

Companies

A company is set up to run a business; It has to be registered before it can start to operate, but once all the paperwork is completed and approved the company becomes recognised as a legal body. The owners of a company are its *shareholders*. However, other individuals and businesses do not deal with the shareholders – they deal with 'the company'. Shareholders put funds into the company by buying shares.

The promoter or directors of the company can apply to the Registrar of Companies for permission to issue new shares. The amount that the Registrar agrees to is called the *authorised capital.*

The *issued capital* is the value of the shares that are actually sold to shareholders. A company may choose not to issue the full value of its authorised capital: it may hold back a certain amount for future issue.

Shares can be issued for payment in stages over a period of time. Each stage is then termed a 'call'. There may be three or four calls before the full price is finally paid. The *paid-up capital* is the money that has been received for these partly-paid shares.

Private companies tend to be smaller than public ones and are often family businesses. There must be at least two shareholders but there is no maximum number. Shares in private companies cannot be traded on the Stock Exchange, and often shares can only be bought with the permission of the *board of directors*.

The board of directors is a committee set up to protect the interests of shareholders. The members of the board choose the managing director, who is responsible for the day-to-day running of the business. The rules of the business set out when shareholders' meetings will take place and the rights of shareholders.

Private companies may find it possible to raise more cash (by sellling shares) than unlimited-liability businesses. The shareholders can also have the protection of limited liability.

The main disadvantages compared with unlimited-liability businesses are that they have to share out profits among shareholders and they cannot make decisions so quickly. They cost more to set up.

A *public company* has its shares bought and sold on the Stock Exchange. Companies can go to the expense of having a 'full quotation' on the Stock Exchange so that their share prices appear on the dealers' visual display screens.

The main advantage of selling shares through the Stock Exchange is that large amounts of capital can be raised very quickly. One disadvantage is that control of business can be lost by the original shareholders if large quantities of shares are purchased as part of a 'takeover bid'. It is also costly to have shares quoted on the Stock Exchange.

In order to create a public company the directors must apply to the Stock Exchange Council, which will carefully check the accounts. A business wanting to 'go public' will then arrange for one of the merchant banks to handle the paperwork. Selling new shares is quite a risky business. The Stock Exchange has 'good days'' (when a lot of people want to buy shares) and 'bad days' (when a lot of people want to sell). If the issue of new shares coincides with a bad day a company can find itself in difficulties. For example, if it hopes to sell a million new shares at £1 each and all goes well, it will raise £1 million; but on a bad day it might only be able to sell half its shares at this price.

One way around this problem is to arrange a 'placing' with a merchant bank. The merchant bank recommends the company's shares to some of the share-buying institutions with which it deals (pension funds and insurance companies, for example) who may then agree to buy, say, one-tenth of the new shares. In this way the merchant bank makes sure that the shares are placed with large investors before the actual date of issue comes round. Then, even if it is a bad day on the Stock Exchange when the shares are issued, the company's money is secure. The shares are therefore 'underwritten' by the merchant bank.

Another common method by which public companies raise capital is to offer new shares for sale to the general public. The company's shares are advertised in leading newspapers and the public are invited to apply. When a company is up and running, a cheaper way of selling is to contact existing shareholders inviting them to buy new shares. This is a *rights issue*.

Adapted from Dave Needham & Robert Dransfield, *Advanced Business*, Oxford: Heinemann, 1995 (pp.118-120)

◇◇ DEFINITIONS ◇◇◇

- **company** a business organisation; *enterprise, firm, business, business concern*
- **shareholder** owner of stock in a company; *stockholder*
- **board of directors** governing body of a corporation responsible for controlling and organizing it in the interests of shareholders
- **unlimited liability businesses** companies for which, if declared bankrupt, the owners have the legal obligation to pay all the debts the companies are unable to meet, even if it means selling nearly all their personal possessions to pay the money that is owed; *partnerships*
- **limited liability businesses** companies for which, if declared bankrupt, the owners have the legal obligation to pay the debts only up to the amount of capital that has been invested in them; *private limited companies* or *public limited companies*.
- **quotation on the stock exchange** official registration of a company with the stock market enabling it to sell shares directly to the public at large; *listing*
- **takeover bid** financial offer made by a firm wanting to buy another one in order to absorb it
- **to underwrite shares** to have a merchant bank's guarantee that it will buy an entire issue of new shares if they remain unsold to the public
- **rights issue** an issue of shares offered first to the exisiting shareholders of a company at less than their market price

◇◇ EXERCISES ◇◇◇

◇ EXERCISE 1 *Comprehension*

Circle the alternative (a), (b) or (c) that most fully and correctly completes the statements or answers the questions below.

1. To set up a company in Britain, the relevant documents have to be sent to
   (a) a merchant bank
   (b) the stock exchange council
   (c) the registrar of companies

2. Who in the company handles the paperwork needed for registration?
   (a) the promoter
   (b) the registrar
   (c) the shareholders

3. What costs most to set up?
   (a) a private limited company
   (b) a family business
   (c) a public limited company

4. Shareholders are safer if they choose to invest in
   (a) a limited liability business
   (b) a family business
   (c) an unlimited liability business

5. The managing director, who is the person responsible for the day-to-day running of the business, is .... by the board of directors
   (a) appointed
   (b) elected
   (c) nominated

6. As part of a takeover bid, the owners of a company can change if
   (a) original shareholders buy a large number of shares at the Stock Exchange
   (b) original shareholders sell a large number of shares at the Stock Exchange
   (c) original shareholders keep a large number of shares at the Stock Exchange

7. The Stock Exchange is the place where companies can raise
   (a) authorised capital
   (b) issued capital
   (c) share capital

8. Selling new shares is quite a risky business for companies because
   (a) it is costly to be quoted on the Stock Exchange
   (b) there is a lot of uncertainty on the Stock Exchange
   (c) there is a lot of paperwork involved

9. To guarantee the issue of new shares, merchant banks usually approach
   (a) other institutional investors
   (b) new shareholders
   (c) existing shareholders

10. Which of the following is a public company in France?
   (a) SNCF
   (b) Renault SA
   (c) Stilnor SARL

◇ EXERCISE 2 *Vocabulary*

(A) Which words or expressions in the text do the phrases below attempt to define?

1. owners of a company ....
2. amount of shares a company can issue ....
3. shares actually sold to shareholders ....
4. one of the stages during which shares can be issued for payment over a period of time ....
5. money received for partly-paid shares ....
6. committee set up to protect the interests of shareholders ....
7. sale of new shares to existing shareholders ....
8. responsibility for company debts ....
9. the details are published in the media so that people can buy ....
10. guaranteed that the shares will be bought if the general public doesn't buy them ..

(B) Match the meanings of the words and expressions in the left-hand column used in the text with those in the right-hand one, some of which are more formal.

1. paperwork	a. initial investors
2. arrange a placing	b. a company being floated
3. up and running	c. find a share-buyer for a company
4. The stock exchange's good days	d. computer monitors
5. The stock exchange's bad days	e. institutional investors
6. a business wanting to go public	f. be quoted
7. visual display screens	g. administrative tasks or formalities
8. original shareholders	h. in full operation
9. share-buying institutions	i. stock market crashes
10. have shares bought and sold on the Stock Exchange	j. stock market's busy days

◇ EXERCISE 3 *Grammar*

Past tenses

(A) We learn in the main text that stock markets and companies can have good and bad days.
Which verbs in the text above suggest a good day and which ones suggest a bad day for stock exchanges and companies?
Put them in the left and right-hand columns respectively.

…………	…………
…………	…………
	…………
	…………

(B) Add the following verbs to the lists

to climb, to crash, to decline, to decrease, to deteriorate, to get better, to get worse, to go down, to go up, to hit bottom, to improve, to increase, to jump, to plunge, to plummet, to rally, to recover, to reach a peak, to peak, to rocket, to slip, to shoot up

…………	…………
…………	…………
…………	…………
…………	…………
…………	…………
…………	…………
…………	…………
…………	…………
…………	…………
…………	…………
…………	…………

(C) Make sentences of your own with these additional verbs, using past tenses

◇ EXERCISE 4 *Assignment*

1. Find out what documents are required to set up a company in your country and where you have to send them.
2. Discuss the findings with your classmates.

FROM THE BUSINESS NEWS

TUG-OF-WAR

Pathé likely to seek listing to fund acquisitions

◇ EXERCISE

Read the article below and discuss or write answers to the following questions

1. What type of company is Pathé?
2. Why do they want to go public?
3. What type of company is Canal Plus?
4. What would Pathé need to envisage buying Canal Plus?
5. What else might prevent Pathé from buying Canal Plus?

Pathé likely to seek listing to fund acquisitions

Pathé, the French media giant, has signalled it is likely to seek a stock market listing in the next 18 months to fund expansion.

Jérôme Seydoux, patriach of the family-owned company, said floating the film distributor and entertainment group was the final thing he wanted to accomplish before he retired. "It depends on market conditions, but don't be surprised if it happened within 18 months", he added.

The move would help raise funds for possible acquisitions. "Today we are a private company and I'm not a great believer in private companies. We would have to go to the market if we needed to raise finances, merge or make an acquisition. I think it would make sense for Pathé to merge with another entertainment company, but at the right time."

Mr Seydoux made clear the group's aspirations to become a force in the domestic television industry. Pathé owns several French cable channels and will enter the country's digital terrestrial market though TMC, which was recently granted a free digital terrestrial television licence by the French government. "I want to become a major player in French television", he said.

While Pathé denied reports that it was part of a Franco-Belgian group of investors looking to buy Canal Plus, the pay-television subsidiary of cash-strapped Vivendi Universal, Mr Seydoux made clear the entertainment group's interests.

"If I can, I would like to own Canal Plus...but for the time being it is not for sale. If it was, and the price was right and I could raise sufficient finances, then who knows?"

A deal to buy Canal Plus would need the approval of Lagardère, the French conglomerate which owns 34 per cent of a unit of the broadcaster. Lagardère is likely to exercise its pre-emptive rights for the unit if Vivendi attempted to sell Canal Plus.

Boyd Farrow and Emilko Terazono,
Financial Times,
Tuesday 5 November 2002 (p.19)

CHAPTER 14

JOB ROLES IN BUSINESS ORGANISATIONS

◇ Key words and concepts

directors
managers
supervisors
human resource management
routine tasks
strategic decisions
organisational structure
layers of command
customers
employees
suppliers
mover and shaker
managing director
executive directors
non-executive directors
policy decisions
budgeting
senior managers / senior management
scope
middle managers
junior managers
operational decisions
backbone of an organisation
at ground level
demanding job
rise through the ranks
cope with
upgraded
operatives
shelf fillers
check out staff
assistant
clerical assistant
kitchen assistant
learning on the job

◇ Vocabulary aid

cutters	coupeuses
stitchers	piqueuses
packers	emballeurs

Instructions For Study

1° Turn to the **definitions** following the text *Job Roles in Business Organisations*. They refer to the specialist terms printed in **bold** type in the list of **Key words and concepts**. Study them closely and pinpoint them in the text.
2° Use an **English** language dictionary to check the meanings (in context) of the other words in the list.
3° Do the exercises to test your comprehension, vocabulary and grammar skills.

Job Roles in Business Organisations

Directors, managers and supervisors all have responsibilities relating to human resource management. Individuals' job roles extend and expand as they progress upwards in an organisation, moving from the handling of daily routine tasks to making strategic decisions.

On the whole, the larger an organisation the more complicated its organisational structure. Large organisations often require several 'layers' of command. Some people spend a lot of time making important decisions while others are mainly involved in carrying out routine tasks and following set procedures.

Directors are individuals with legal responsibility to the business's customers, employees, suppliers and shareholders. It is the directors who generally make the strategic decisions in a business or organisation.

The Board of Directors is thus the top level of a company. Directors sit on the board because they have specialist expertise in a particular line of business, or because they have generalist business experience or sometimes more importantly, good contacts.

People are 'approached' by a company to become directors, though their appointment must be approved by shareholders. The Board of Directors will usually include a financial expert, an expert with detailed knowledge of the product or service concerned, an expert in getting things done ('a mover and shaker'), a marketing expert, someone with a lot of contacts, and other key directors depending on the business or industry.

The Managing Director is the head of the organisation. He or she needs to be a person of considerable influence, intelligence, and with the ability to get the board to work together and in the right direction. When choosing directors it may be wise to appoint someone who is also a director of a variety of other companies in order to draw on their general experience. Politicians are also often invited to be directors because of their political influence.

A distinction is often made between 'executive directors' and 'non-executive directors'. Executive directors are those who are directly involved in the day-today running of the organisation, taking a responsibility for 'executing' decisions. Non-executive directors are influential directors who will simply attend board meetings. The non-executive directors bring to the business extra experience and influence. As a company moves on into new fields and production lines, some directors will no longer be required while new directors with different skills will be taken on.

Managers have the job of deploying an organisation's resources and making policy decisions. Managers use and develop systems for 'organising the organisation'. This involves deciding on objectives, making decisions to ensure that the objectives are met, and then planning, organising and coordinating activities. The manager's function is particularly concerned with bringing together sets of activities and tasks which contribute towards the completion of whole projects. It also involves controlling, i.e. making sure that things are going to plan. Of course, budgeting is a key aspect of management. That is, the manager must be able to forecast incomings and outgoings from the organisation in order to better control finance and other resources.

However, research into what managers actually do presents us with a slightly different picture. Most managers in the real world spend a lot of time chasing after things, and reacting to events after they have happened. This is often because the work environment is so fast moving and unpredictable that it is difficult to predict future events.

Managers therefore need to be highly alert and be able to make quick and appropriate decisions. The great quality of an effective manager is the ability to get on with people and to be able to influence people to work in a positive direction. Managers also need to be healthy and have the ability to absorb pressure.

Strategic or senior managers make top-level decisions concerning the scope of an organisation's activities. These decisions set out what the managers want an organisation to be like and to be about. Strategic decisions are therefore vital for the development and welfare of an organisation. They require detailed analysis and considerable use of skilled judgement.

Examples of strategic decisions include deciding to develop a new product, to open up new markets, or to carry out major investment projects. Of course many of these strategic decisions will need to be approved at the Board of Directors level. Some top managers will have a dual role as directors.

Middle managers organise and control the resources of an organisation within established guidelines. Middle managers do, however, usually have considerable scope for using their own judgement and for bringing in new ideas after consultation with senior management.

Examples of middle management decisions include setting out and controlling a departmental budget, organising a sales force, and changing prices of products in reponse to changes in the market.

Junior managers are usually concerned with short-term operational decisions, as well as longer-term ones. Operational decisions are routine and frequently recurring tasks that can be carried out following straightforward rules. Examples include managing stock, arranging schedules for the delivery of goods, and organising hours worked by staff.

Supervisors are quite often the backbone of an organisation. They are people who know how things should be done at 'ground level'. They work with middle and junior managers to put plans into practice at an operational level.

Supervisors know the capabilities of all resources (machines, people and materials) because they work in among them every day.

Supervision is a skilled and demanding job. The supervisor is like a sergeant major in the army giving orders to the ground troops. He or she will be first in line to deal with day-to-day problems as and when they occur.

Organisations therefore look for people with good qualifications to fill supervisory roles. They are likely to have mathematical and communication skills as well as a good knowledge of the technology of their industry, including information technology.

Supervisors may have risen 'through the ranks' of their organisation by hard work and the ability to cope with responsibility, so they need to have their skills periodically upgraded through training courses.

Whilst operational activities may be routine, they need to be done with great care and precision. There are many types of operatives. In a supermaket there are shelf fillers and check-out staff; in a textile company there are cutters, stitchers and packers; etc.

Operators need to feel that they are valued, and there should be opportunities for them to learn new skills, so that they can move on to higher grade work. The word operative is sometimes used to describe someone who works on a machine, or someone who has a particular skill.

The term assistant is also frequently used in business to describe someone who helps others to carry out their work effectively. For example, the terms clerical assistant, dental assistant, and kitchen assistant are used commonly.

The assistant will carry out very routine operations but during this process will be learning 'on the job'. The work of an assistant is very important. Without assistants, work could not be carried out to a high standard.

Dave Needam & Robert Dransfield, *Advanced Business*,
Oxford: Heinemann, 1995, (pp.340–343)

◇◇ DEFINITIONS ◇◇◇

- **directors** individuals in a company who generally make strategic decisions and who are responsible by law to the business's customers, employees, suppliers and shareholders
- **managers** individuals in a company, in charge of deploying resources and making policy decisions by planning, organising, staffing, directing, coordinating and budgeting the activities of the firm; *executives*
- **supervisors** employees who oversee and direct the work of others; *foremen*
- **human resource management** creation, development and maintenance of an effective workforce, matching the requirements of the organisation and responding to the environment; *personnel management*
- **organisational structure** the way employees are grouped in an organisation *viz*, by function, product, process, geographical area or by type of customer; *organisation chart, organogram*
- **customers** people or companies buying goods and/or services. Satisfying their needs is the key purpose of all business organisations; *clients*
- **employees** people paid for working for an organisation; *workers, staff, personnel, workforce*
- **suppliers** private individuals or companies providing resources of all kinds to other companies such as raw materials, components, capital goods, funds or personnel
- **mover and shaker** director in a company who has excellent communication skills and who is an expert in getting things done
- **managing director** person with the ultimate responsibility for a business organisation and its operations; *Chief Executive Officer (CEO)*
- **budgeting** forecasting incomings and outgoings from the organisation in order to better control finance and other resources
- **operatives** workers employed in a factory usually operating (controlling and using) a machine or apparatus; *operators*
- **assistant** someone who helps others to carry out their work effectively

◇◇ EXERCISES ◇◇◇

◇ EXERCISE 1 *Comprehension*

(A) True / False Circle the correct choice and justify your answer

1. All directors have supervisory roles in companies T / F
2. A good board of directors is ideally made up of members with complementary skills and expertise T / F
3. Non-executive directors are usually influential people who bring customers to the business T / F
4. In practice most managers' jobs involve planning, organising, coordinating and/or controlling activities T / F

5. Strategic decisions are made by executive rather than non-executive directors T / F
6. Drawing up schedules for staff for example would be the responsibility of a middle manager in an organisation T / F
7. Supervisors are sometimes former shop floor workers who have been promoted through experience and training T / F
8. Operators are different from operatives in that they work only on machines T / F
9. The job positions described in the text are found at different levels of management T / F
10. The job roles described in the text suggest a clear-cut hierarchy in large organisations T / F

(B) Who's who in the organisation?

Here is a number of job positions listed in alphabetical order. Where would you put them in the organisational structure below of a fictitious large company? Put the corresponding number next to the job position.

bending machine operator ( ) cutting machine operator ( ) cost controller ( ) financial director ( ) fork lift truck operator ( ) Human resource director ( ) human resource manager ( ) marketing director ( ) managing director ( ) production director ( ) plant manager A ( ) plant manager B ( ) plant manager C ( ) quality manager ( ) research and development director ( ) shift supervisor A ( ) shift supervisor B ( ) shift supervisor C ( ) works manager ( ) welding machine operator ( )

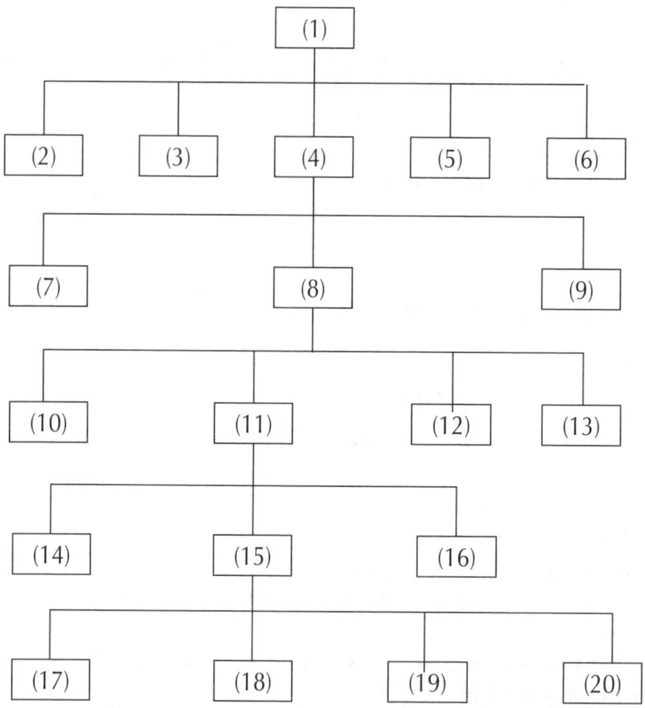

◇ EXERCISE 2 *Vocabulary*

(A) Find sentences in the text with equivalent terms to the words and expressions in *italics* below.

1. Individuals' job roles extend and expand as they *progress upwards in an organisation*, moving from the *handling of daily routine tasks* to making strategic decisions.
2. Some people spend a lot of time making important decisions while others are maily involved in *carrying out* routine tasks.
3. When choosing directors it may be wise to *appoint* someone who is also a director of a variety of other companies.
4. Operational decisions are routine and frequently *recurring tasks* that can be carried out following *straightforward rules*

(B) Find words or expressions in the text which mean or refer to the following.

1. levels of management ....
2. business activity ....
3. to implement decisions ....
4. cashiers ....
5. challenging work ....
6. stockholders ....
7. earnings ....
8. expenses ....

◇ EXERCISE 3 *Grammar*

Verbs in action

(A) Below are 10 expressions you might like to use if you wish to describe job roles in a company:

X deals with Y ; X is concerned with Y ; X reports to Y ;
X is responsible for Y ; X is responsible to Y : X supervises Y ;
X manages Y ; X oversees Y ; X is in charge of Y ; X handles Y.

1. Which expressions would you use to suggest that someone is in command?
2. Which expressions would you use to suggest that someone receives orders?
3. Which expressions would you use to simply describe what a person does in the organisation?

(B) Now make ten sentences of your own with each of these expressions to describe relationships in the organisation chart you completed in exercise 1 **(B)** above.

◇ EXERCISE 4 *Assignment*

Visit the website of a company you have heard about. Find information on the people who work for the organisation and the positions they hold. Draw an organogram of the company and describe it to the class.

FROM THE BUSINESS NEWS

CHIEF EXECUTIVES

The curse of charisma

◇ EXERCISE

Read the article below and discuss or write answers to the following questions

1. Why do companies tend to recruit charismatic CEOs?
2. Is there a correlation between a CEO's charisma and company performance?
3. What type of CEOs are hired as replacements for departing charismatic ones?
4. What impact, if any, does a replacement Chief Executive Officer have on a company's performance?
5. Why is a CEOs' charisma described to be a curse for companies?

The curse of charisma

Look round the new faces in the boardroom these days: few have been selected for glamour. They are folks such as Glenn Tilton, brought in this week from ChevronTexaco to rescue United Airlines and described as " extremely hardworking "; Edward Breen, a safe pair of hands from Motorola who is trying to unscramble the mess left by Dennis Kozlowski at Tyco; or Sir Nick Scheele, chief operating officer at Ford and a solid contrast to the excessively colourful Jacques Nasser. Safe is in, charisma is out.

About time too. A flurry of research casts doubt on the value of charismatic leadership. In the latest issue of the *Harvard Business Review*, Ralesh Khurana of Harvard Business School argues that firms appoint charismatic bosses because they tend to believe- despite a notable lack of conclusive evidence- that a chief executive can have an almost mystical impact on a company's performance. In fact, he says, most studies suggest that 10-20% of performance depends on the economic climate and 30-45% on the state of the industry.(That still leaves 35-60%, however.)

Belief in the clout of bosses also encourages companies to dump them when things go badly. So tenure at the top grows ever briefer. And when the boss goes, companies frequently hire a charismatic outsider to save them, often somebody from a high-profile stable such as Citigroup (James Dimon at Bank One) or

General Electric (John Trani at Stanley Works).

Dismissal now accounts for 37% of all departures of chief executives. Firms that sack the boss are roughly three times as likely as others to hire an outsider as a replacement. However, argues Margarethe Wiersema of the University of California at Irvine, in a paper presented at last month's annual meeting of the Academy of Management, replacement chief executives are no better than their predecessors at improving performance. The newcomer makes little difference to either profits or the share price.

Only in one respect does charisma demonstrably pay. Another Academy of Management paper, by Henry Tosi of the University of Florida, assessed the charisma of the chief executives of 59 large American firms and duly found no connection with corporate performance. It did, however, find that charismatic bosses receive higher total pay than their humbler peers, after discounting both company size and performance. Charisma, it seems, is as good for the boss as it is bad for shareholders.

The Economist , 7 September 2002 (p.70)

CHAPTER 15

MERGERS AND ACQUISITIONS IN THE EUROPEAN UNION

◇ Key words and concepts

mergers
acquisitions
mergers and acquisitions
European Union
euro-companies
monopolistic advantages
European Commission
Merger Control Regulation
joint venture
ECU
impede
cross border deals
global players
marketplace

Instructions For Study

1° Turn to the **definitions** following the text *Mergers and Acquisitions in the European Union.* They refer to the specialist terms printed in bold type in the list of **Key words and concepts.** Study them closely and pinpoint them in the text.
2° Use an English language dictionary to check the meanings (in context) of the other words in the list.
3° Do the exercises to test your comprehension, vocabulary and grammar skills.

Mergers and Acquisitions in the European Union

Mergers and acquisitions within the European Union (EU) can be viewed from two perspectives: first, they can be seen as a necessary step to the development of *Euro-companies* – firms with the necessary size and resources to compete with other international giants – and second, they can be regarded as attempts to gain monopolistic advantages leading to reduced intra-European competition and higher prices.

The control given to the European Commission (EC) under the Merger Control Regulation came into effect in 1990 and sought to remove the need for companies to clear a merger or acquisition through both national and EC authorities. The EC requires notification of a merger within one week of its announcement and judges its merits on the basis of answers to three questions:

1. Does the proposed merger, acquisition or joint venture create a concentration resulting in a single autonomous entity?
2. Does the proposed merger have an effect on the EU? Specifically, does the concentration have annual global sales or more than ECU 5 billion and are the EU-wide sales more than ECU 250 million? If each party derives more than two-thirds of its total sales from one country it will come under national competition policy rather than EU regulation. The global threshold may fall to ECU 2 billion in 1994 to tighten the Commission's control over EU mergers and acquisitions.
3. Does the new concentration impede competition? This criterion, which requires a larger element of judgement, reflects the potentially harmful consequences of mergers which place the new organization in a position to exploit market power to the detriment of its customers.

A wave of merger activity preceded the creation of the Single Market. Cross-border deals involving EU companies from 1988 to 1992 peaked in 1989 at ECU 41 billion but had fallen to half that level by 1991. Merger activity in 1992 was estimated at ECU 312 billion. Most activity was in financial services with deals totalling ECU 25 billion during this period. Most notable was the Hongkong & Shangai Bank's acquisition of the Midland Bank.

The food, drink and tobacco sector also saw much activity ($28 billion), an example being Nestlé's acquisition of Rowntree MacIntosh. The third busiest sector was electrical and electronics ($20 billion) with Whirlpool of the USA acquiring Philips's white goods (washing machines, refrigerators, etc.) business in 1992, and Maytag, also from the USA, buying Hoover in 1989, for example.

Clearly some of this activity is driven by European companies wishing to establish themselves as global players in the markets they serve, while other acquisitions are motivated by a desire to establish a presence in the Single Market. Whatever the drive, acquisition and merger is seen as a major strategic weapon for companies seeking to build their businesses in an increasingly competitive marketplace.

David Jobber, *Principles and Practice of Marketing*, Maidenhead (UK): McGraw-Hill Publishing Company, 1998 (p.543)

◇◇ DEFINITIONS ◇◇◇

- ♦ **merger** combination of two companies to form a new one. A merger is *horizontal* when two companies supplying the same sort of product or service combine; *vertical* when companies supplying a product at different stages of production combine or *conglomerate* when companies that produce quite different products combine
- ♦ **acquisition** situation in which one firm buys a controlling interest in another through the purchase of its shares, the target firm usually maintaining its identity as a subsidiary company; *takeover, buyout*
- ♦ **mergers and acquisitions** strategic alliances companies make by combining with or buying others in order to increase their grip on the market they trade in; *M&A*
- ♦ **monopolistic advantages** benefits companies enjoy when controlling the entire manufacturing and selling of a product or the entire provision of a service
- ♦ **joint venture** cooperation by two or more parties on a business project, which may or may not involve the creation of a separate company
- ♦ **ECU (European Currency Unit)** monetary standard formerly used for comparing the value of European hard currencies. It has since been replaced by the euro.
- ♦ **cross-border deals** alliances and / or transactions made by companies from different countries
- ♦ **marketplace** trading conditions; *business environment*

◇◇ EXERCISES ◇◇◇

◇ EXERCISE 1 *Comprehension*

Answer these questions

1. What are the reasons why companies decide to merge with or acquire other firms?
2. How did the creation of the Single Market influence merger activity? Has this activity ceased?
3. Why was 1992 a crucial date? What happened then?
4. Which sectors were particularly prone to mergers and acquisitions?
5. What role does the European Commission play in the field of mergers and acquisitions?
6. Which institutions supervise or control merger activity?
7. What potential dangers are associated with mergers, acquisitions and joint ventures?

◇ EXERCISE 2 *Vocabulary*

What do the following phrases mean? Use your own words.

1. can be viewed ....
2. to clear a merger or acquisition through both national and EC authorities ....
3. a single autonomous entity ....
4. global sales ....

5. global threshold ....
6. global players ....
7. impede competition ....
8. cross border deals peaked ....
9. this activity is driven by ....
10. whatever the drive ....

◇ EXERCISE 3 *Grammar*

The Simple Past

(A) 1. Underline all the verbs used in the text you have just studied.
2. Which verbs are regular and which ones are irregular?
3. Give the infinitive form of the irregular verbs you have identified.

(B) Using your own sentences, retell the events that took place on the European mergers and acquisitions market at the dates below.Use the simple past tense.

1. From 1998 to 1992 ....
2. 1989 ....
3. 1990 ....
4. 1991 ....
5. 1992 ....
6. 1994 ....

◇ EXERCISE 4 *Discussion*

Does «bigger» necessarily mean «better» for firms?

FROM THE BUSINESS NEWS

ELECTRIC SHOCK

At last, a single market (maybe)

◇ EXERCISE

Read the article below and discuss or write answers to the following questions

1. What shows that the move towards a single market in Europe has been slow?
2. Which economic sector is going to be liberalised by 2004 and 2007?
3. Do you know anything about other recent market openings?
4. Is there a case of unfair competition in the text?
5. Where do the benefits and drawbacks of liberalisation lie as far as companies and consumers ar concerned?

At last, a single market (maybe)

The single European market was introduced to great fanfare in 1992. In reality, though, creating a single market for goods and services within the European Union is a process, not an event – and a very slow moving process it can be. In recent years, the single biggest goal of the liberalisers has been to force a faster opening of the European markets for electricity and gas. Together, these account for over 250 billion worth ($250 billion) of sales every year in the EU. Yet market-opening has been lopsided. The British and Finnish markets are fully open, for example, but all French domestic users still have to buy electricity from their state monopoly, Electricité de France (EDF).

On November 25th European ministers finally agreed a date for complete liberalisation across the EU. All business users will be free to choose energy suppliers by July 2004, and this right will be extended to all domestic users in 2007. The French, who blocked any such agreement at recent European summits, have changed their position. France had found itself increasingly isolated in its efforts to slow liberalisation. And the interests of EDF, a state-owned giant that is Europe's biggest electricity supplier, now point in the direction of market-opening.

That is because EDF has ambitious goals for international expansion. It had run into a political backlash after recent takeover bids in Italy and Spain. Politicians there had complained that it was unfair to let EDF expand into other European markets, so long as the French market remained closed. That objection will now lose some of its force.

The German energy market may also change as a result of the new EU decision. In theory, the German market is already 100% liberalised. But new entrants have complained that they have been held back by regulatory obstacles. These too will be tackled, at least in theory (though in both France and Germany, it remains to be seen just what happens in practice).

The two biggest consequences of energy liberalisation are likely to be cheaper prices and a wave of corporate mergers, maybe even across European borders. Both effects have already been felt in Britain, since competition was introduced to energy business. Electricity prices for big consumers have fallen by around 40% in Britain since 1998; 34% of Britons have changed providers; and 55% of British households now get electricity from a foreign-owned company. Companies from other European countries have expanded rapidly in Britain. EDF bought London Electricity in 1998 and Seeboard in 2002, and is now the fourth-biggest electricity supplier in Britain.

This week ENI, an Italian energy company, announced a € 2.5 billion bid to take complete control of Italgas (it currently owns 44% of the company). ENI's management cited a desire to take advantage of the renewed impetus for energy liberalisation across Europe as a key motive for the bid. Other energy companies are thinking of making similar moves. Gaz de France has announced ambitious plans to expand internationally and EDF will continue its expansion drive. Observers of the European energy market believe, gloomily, that it may ultimately come to be dominated by three large, well-entrenched national champions: EDF, and the two German companies, RWE and E.ON.

The Economist, 30 November 2002, (p.58)

CHAPTER 16

FEATURES OF MULTINATIONAL ENTERPRISES

◇ Key words and concepts

features
multinational enterprises
headquarters
operations
trade
investment
globalisation
environments
competitors
resources
assets
trademarks
patents
designs
glass maker
process
licensing
royalties
expertise
decentralised
subsidiaries
centralised
targets
product range
packaging

Instructions For Study

1° Turn to the **definitions** following the text *Features of Multinational Enterprises*. They refer to the specialist terms printed in **bold** type in the list of **Key words and concepts**. Study them closely and pinpoint them in the text.
2° Use an **English** language dictionary to check the meanings (in context) of the other words in the list.
3° Do the exercises to test your comprehension, vocabulary and grammar skills

Features of Multinational Enterprises

The MNE is an enterprise that has its headquarters in one place, the home country, but has operations in others (the host countries). Note that this is a form of international business in that it is involved both in trade and investment across frontiers. The MNE harnesses the twin forces of globalisation and technology to achieve its ends. From this statement we can derive three key characteristics of these organisations:

■ MNEs must respond to environments in both their home and host countries. Many aspects are replicated from country to country. For example, in the operating environment, globalisation of markets means that an MNE will meet the same competitors in each nation or region.This applies as much to Sony and Toshiba as it does to BP and Royal Dutch/Shell. Yet different traditions and histories of competition, combined with the presence of local competitors, can have subtle or substantial effects.

The wider environment also has a variable influence. For instance, the way products are used varies from place to place. Germans prefer to wash clothes in very hot water while Brazilians wash their clothes (and themselves) in cold. This distinction, with variations in water quality and other factors, means that the soaps and detergents on sale are not the same.

■ The strength of the MNE is drawn from its pool of resources. These range from the tangible assets of plant and facilities to the intangible assets of information, trademarks, patents and designs. Capital can be made available for projects and, given the general strength of the business, funds can be obtained at advantageous rates. Furthermore, there are the knowledge and skills of the personnel. They know how to supply and make things, how to buy and sell. Many international developments are based on applying the knowledge in new markets. Pilkington, the glass maker based in North-West England, gained a technological advantage from its float glass process. It used a system of licensing, followed by direct investment, to ensure rapid and widespread application of its knowledge while it was protected by patents. The flow of royalties enabled it to become one of the world's leading glass companies. At a smaller scale, Glenmorangie's entry to China and India is based on its process expertise.

■ The MNE can plan and control all its resources. Sometimes it can do this in a decentralised manner, allowing local subsidiaries to work closely with their environments. In other cases it is very centralised, setting targets and making detailed plans from headquarters. Development of global products, from Proton Cars to Pepsi-Cola tends to be centralised. At the other extreme, the managers and editors of newspapers in the News International Group are expected to fit them to the needs of local markets. Lego for example decided to change the balance between global and local as it found it needed to adapt its product range and packaging to suit local needs.

John Naylor, *Management*,
London: Financial Times / Pitman Publishing, 1999 (p.138)

◇◇ DEFINITIONS ◇◇◇

♦ **multinational enterprise** enterprise that has its headquarters in one place, the home country, but has operations in others, the host countries; *transnational enterprise* or *transnational corporation*
♦ **investment** buying the machinery and equipment to make used goods or needed to provide services
♦ **globalisation** internationalising, harmonising, standardising and controlling the production of goods and services on a worldwide basis
♦ **environments** natural, economic, legal, social or political surroundings of a company which have an influence on its operations
♦ **competitors** firms which are rivals in business; *business rivals*
♦ **assets** items that are owned by an organisation or money and other items that are owed to the organisation. The items owned can be *tangible* such as buildings and machinery or *intangible* such as intellectual property; *resources*
♦ **trademarks** signs that can identify the products of one business from those of another. These can be a word, a device, a three-dimensional shape, a sound or a smell
♦ **patents** documents showing the protection granted by governments giving someone or a company the exclusive rights to manufacture, sell or use an invention or new industrial process over a particular number of years
♦ **process** procedure, flow of activities, sequence of tasks
♦ **licensing** granting a *licence*, i.e. an official document which gives one permission to produce or market a product or service within an agreed area for a specific time, in return for a fee. A company selling a licence is a *licensor* and a firm buying one is a *licensee*
♦ **royalties** payments made to writers, inventors and owners of property everytime their books, devices and land are bought or used by others
♦ **subsidiaries** companies owned and controlled by other big, usually multinational, enterprises

◇◇ EXERCISES ◇◇◇

◇ EXERCISE 1 *Comprehension*

(A) Select the names of eight multinational companies in the text and fill in the relevant information in the grid below

Company	Home country	Sector of industry

(B) Answer these questions

1. What are the main activities of MNEs?
2. What means do MNEs have at their disposal to sustain their activities?
3. What does the strength of MNEs depend on?
4. How can MNEs control their resources?
5. How do MNEs transfer technology across frontiers?

◇ EXERCISE 2 ***Vocabulary***

(A) Use the list of definitions above **to select the appropriate term**, in its singular or plural form, to fit each sentence.

1. The .... side of a balance sheet is normally set out in what is called an inverse order of liquidity.
2. If you are producing a manufactured product such as biscuits you will need to design a .... which takes account of factors such as size, shape, texture, colour or flavour.
3. Suppliers are able to get funds for .... by borrowing money from private individuals, banks and other financial institutions.
4. Faced with pressure from .... in low cost countries, companies usually automate and rationalise much of their operations.
5. .... of trade increases the importance of protecting intellectual property in many countries.
6. Since early 1996, the Patent Office of the United Kingdom has permitted individuals to register their own names as ...., provided they are distinctive enough.
7. Once a company has become a ...., it will set up operations in different countries and engage in international trade.
8. Home-country managers are seldom placed in top positions in overseas ....
9. A grave danger of .... is the loss of product and process know-how to third parties who may become competitors once the agreement is at an end.
10. The economic .... can have a critical impact on the success of companies through its effect on supply and demand.

(B) Find words or expressions in the text which mean the following

1. characteristics ....
2. head office ....
3. the country in which a multinational enterprise is/was created ....
4. buying and selling ....
5. worldwide ....
6. to reach its objectives ....
7. glass company ....
8. know-how ....
9. fixing specific objectives ....
10. portfolio ....

◇ EXERCISE 3 ***Grammar***

Noun formation

(A) Look up in the list of definitions above the range of nouns which can be formed from the verb ***to license***

(B) Complete the text below with a noun stemming from the verb *to license*

...........(1) refers to contracts in which a foreign ....(2) provides a local ....(3) with access to one or a set of technologies or know-how in exchange for financial compensation. The ....(4) will normally have exclusive rights to produce and market the product within an agreed area for a specific period of time in return for a *royalty* based on sales volume. A ....(5) may relate to the use of patent for either a product or process, copyright, trade marks and trade secrets (e.g. designs and software) and know-how (e.g. product and process specifications).
...........(6) agreements allow the exporter to enter markets that otherwise may be closed for exports or other forms of market entry without the need to make substantial capital investments in the host country. However, control of production is lost and the reputation of the ....(7) is dependent on the performance of the ....(8). A grave danger of ....(9) is the loss of product and process know-how to third parties who may become competitors once the agreement is at an end.
The need to exploit new technology simultaneously in many markets has stimulated the growth in ....(10) by small high tech companies which lack the resources to set up their own sales and market offices, engage in joint ventures or conduct direct investment abroad. ....(11) is also popular in R&D-intensive industries such as pharmaceuticals, chemicals and synthetic fibres, where rising research and development costs have encouraged ....(12) as a form of reciprocal technology exchange. In Europe, ...(13) is encouraged by the European Union, which seeks the mechanism as a way of offering access to new technologies to companies without the resources to innovate and provide a means of technology sharing on a pan-European scale. ....(14) activities have been given exemption in EU competition law, which means that companies engaged in ....(15) cannot be accused of anticompetitive practices, and *tied purchase* agreements whereby ....(16) must buy components from the ....(17) have not been ruled anticompetitive since they allow the innovating firm protection from loss of know-how to other component suppliers.

David Jobber, *Principles and Pratice of Marketing*, 2nd edition,
London: McGraw-Hill Publishing Company, 1998 (p. 653)

◇ EXERCISE 4 ***Discussion***

What is your understanding of the word ***environment(s)*** in the following sentences found in the text?

1. MNEs must respond to *environments* in both their home and host countries.
2. For example, in the operating *environment*, globalisation of markets means that an MNE will meet the same competitors in each nation or region.
3. The wider *environment* also has a variable influence.
4. Sometimes it can do this in a decentralised manner, allowing local subsidiaries to work closely with their *environments*.

CENTRALIZATION VERSUS DECENTRALIZATION IN TRANSNATIONAL CORPORATIONS

◊ Key words and concepts

centralization
decentralization
transnational corporation
environment
global integration
regional responsiveness
economies of scale
marketing profile
channel intermediaries
advertising
packaging
labelling
pricing
not invented here syndrome
customization of products
brand
brand positioning
retailer
responsibility
blend
resentment
parent company
board meetings
annual report

Instructions For Study

1° Turn to the **definitions** following the text *Centralization versus Decentralization in Transnational Corporations*. They refer to the specialist terms printed in **bold** type in the list of **Key words and concept**. Study them closely and pinpoint them in the text.
2° Use an **English** language dictionary to check the meanings (in context) of the other words in the list.
3° Do the exercises to test your comprehension, vocabulary and grammar skills

Centralization versus Decentralization in Transnational Corporations

A key determinant of the way international operations are organized is the degree to which the environment calls for global integration (centralization) versus regional responsiveness (decentralization). *Centralization* reaps economies of scale and provides an integrated marketing profile to channel intermediaries who themselves may be international, and customers who are increasingly geographically mobile. Confusion over product formulations, advertising approaches, packaging design and labelling, and pricing is eliminated by a coordinated approach. (However, too much centralization can lead to the *not invented here syndrome* where managers in one country are slow to introduce products that have been successful in others, or fail to fully support advertising campaigns that have been conceived elsewhere.)

Decentralization maximises customization of products to regional tastes and preferences. Since decentralized decision-making is closer to customers, speed of response to new opportunities is quicker than with a centralized organizational structure. Relationships with the trade and government are facilitated by local decision-making.

Many companies feel the pressure of both sets of forces, hence the development of the transnational corporation. European integration has led many companies to review their overseas operations with the objective of realizing global economies wherever possible. European centralized marketing teams carry the responsibility for looking at the longer-term strategic picture alongside national marketing staff who deal less with advertising theme development and brand positioning and more with handling retailer relationships. The result is loss of responsibility and power for national marketing managers. This is a sensitive issue and many companies are experimenting with the right blend of centralization and national power. Desire to preserve national identity and resentment of centralized European interference can run deep.

One British company, owned by a German parent for more than a decade, still battled to preserve its national identity by holding its own formal board meetings and publishing its own separate annual report. When Pampers was launched across Europe by Procter and Gamble, an employee found that 'as soon as it was known that I was from the European Technical Centre... my local support dried up'.

David Jobber, *Principles and Practice of Marketing*,
Maidenhead (U.K): McGraw-Hill Publishing Company, 1998 (pp.668-669)

◇◇ DEFINITIONS ◇◇◇

♦ **centralization** management approach in which authority, responsibility, decisions and services of an MNE are controlled by people near the top of the organisation at the headquarters

♦ **decentralization** management approach in which some authority is passed down to managers in the subsidiaries of an MNE who make decisions in response to their local environment

♦ **economies of scale** reduction in the unit cost of products achieved as a result of an increase in the size of the organisation or in the output or again as a result of better technology, management and business practices

♦ **channel intermediaries** firms which facilitate the distribution of products to customers

♦ **pricing** the setting or fixing by a business enterprise of the prices for its goods or services or a company policy on prices

♦ **customization of products** process by which an organisation offers unique products to satisfy the particular needs of customers

♦ **brand** trade name used to identify goods and services in order to distinguish them from competing ones

♦ **brand positioning** differentiating one's brands from those of competitors in a particular market

♦ **retailer** person or firm involved in the activity of selling goods and services in small units directly to the final consumer

♦ **parent company** a company, usually an MNE, which owns and controls other smaller companies; *holding company*

◇◇ EXERCISES ◇◇◇

◇ EXERCISE 1 *Comprehension*

True / False Circle the correct choice and justify your answer

1. In a centralised organisation, the coordination of business activities encourages inefficiencies. T / F
2. In a decentralized business, local managers can react to changes in customer behaviour more quickly. T / F
3. In a multinational enterprise, there is a need for a centralised rather than a decentralised approach. T / F
4. In some European multinational companies, group marketing managers deal with long-term strategies on advertising for example, while national marketing managers deal with day-to-day contacts with local retailers. T / F
5. To avoid losing control of their subsidiaries, European multinational firms are reinforcing their power of centralisation. T / F
6. Some European subsidiaries refuse being centrally controlled by their parent companies. T / F

7. When the idea of launching a new product comes from head office, managers in the subsidiaries are always enthusiastic about marketing the product. T / F
8. In a centralised business, there is more responsibility and power for local managers. T / F
9. Formal board meetings are normally held at headquarters. T / F
10. Achieving a fair balance between centralisation and decentralisation is the best recommendation for MNEs. T / F

◇ EXERCISE 2 *Vocabulary*

Which terms in the text do the following sentences or expressions refer to?

1. It is a document large companies publish once a year which consists of a chairman's statement, a statement of profit and loss account and an auditors' report ....
2. Directors gather on these occasions and discuss matters of importance to the company ....
3. Individuals or firms operating between producers and ultimate consumers. They can be wholesalers or retailers ....
4. Reluctance by local managers to introduce policies or products made elsewhere ....
5. Subsidiaries, branches, offices or other activities located far away from the home country ....
6. Ability to react or make decisions locally in line with developments in the local environment ....
7. Ensuring that company activities across frontiers are standardised and harmonised ....
8. Designing, developing and marketing products ....
9. A delicate topic to talk about ....
10. Feeling of anger or dislike ....

◇ EXERCISE 3 *Grammar*

Noun formation

Complete the following sentences with nouns formed from the following verbs

cannibalise, centralise, commercialise, customise, decentralise, globalise, harmonise, organise, specialise, standardise

1. .... are developed around the principle that work is done more efficiently when employees specialise.
2. Companies can put in place some sort of .... by region or type of customer.
3. Many MNEs implement policies of .... hoping that they can recruit more capable employees.
4. The .... costs of the means of production and services are sometimes high.

5. The development of Information Technology has shifted the balance towards .... as improved communications have enhanced co-ordination amongst staff.
6. The .... of products is a luxury that most customers cannot afford.
7. The trend towards increased integration of business activities throughout the world is known as ....
8. .... is achieved when managers succeed in publishing instructions that workers must follow
9. Companies expanding extensively such as Richard Branson's Virgin company run the risk of ...., a situation in which a new brand gains sales to the detriment of an established brand
10. The marketing department of a company is in charge of developing effective .... strategies for new products.

◇ EXERCISE 4 ***Discussion***

The sentences below are **arguments for** Centralisation or Decentralisation. Sort them out. Write **(C)** in the space provided if you think the argument is in favour of Centralisation and **(D)** if it is for Decentralisation.

1. prevents parts of a company from becoming too independent and thus making decisions which might not fit in with the firm's policies ( )
2. provides staff with more authority ( )
3. makes coordination and management control easier ( )
4. makes it possible for a company to have a common policy ( )
5. gives employees a chance to broaden their experience ( )
6. improves economies of scale and reduces overheads ( )
7. improves the speed of decision making ( )
8. improves the morale and motivation of staff who have greater ability to make decisions affecting their activities ( )
9. enables decisions to be made at a level which is closer to the point where they are needed ( )
10. allows more flexibility ( )

FROM THE BUSINESS NEWS

BETTER STANDARDS

Ethically unemployed

◇ EXERCISE

Read the article below and discuss or write answers to the following questions

1. What shows that Reebok is an MNE?
2. Why has the company decided to withdraw from Thailand?

3. What is a sweatshop?
4. Do you think Reebok is a centralised or decentralised organisation?
5. What difference is the writer making between social responsibility and social irresponsibility?

Ethically unemployed

How little the dangerous fashion for corporate social responsibility has to do with a truly responsible attitude by businesses is aptly shown by Reebok International. This American sports-goods supplier claims to have pioneered good corporate practice.

Doug Cahn, the company's head of human rights, talks about values, fairness and principles, with all the zeal of an anti-corporate lobbyist. He presents the news that Reebok has just decided to withdraw business from a subcontracted factory in Thailand as a proof of corporate caring. The reason: the 400 or so workers employed there to make shorts and shirts were working for more than 72 hours a week.

It is responsible to press for better standards, but the supply of good jobs matters too. Workers at this Bangkok factory were paid above the minimum wage, with health-and-safety rights that few local manufacturers would offer. Many factory employees in developing countries want to work more hours rather than fewer.

Although Mr Cahn denies it, the company seems to have pulled out to avoid allegations that it was doing business with what critics call a sweatshop. "There are always people outside who want to talk with our factory workers to check our standards," he says. Reebok has been stung before. One troublesome former factory worker in Hong Kong, Hang Dong-fang, hosts a radio show calling for workers to telephone with their complaints. "He is a lightning rod for criticism," says Mr Cahn, before adding quickly that "criticism is one of Reebok's most valuable resources."

Reebok may not have done its shareholders a favour either. If a clean corporate image boosted sales in the developed markets, it might be worth paying the price of finding a new factory. Yet astonishingly, given Reebok's long involvement in ethical trading, it does not research to correlate social responsibility with sales or shareholder value, says Mr Cahn. Nor does he know what his division costs the company. Since the most ethical way to do business is to attract investment and offer more people a way out of peasant labour, perhaps this practice should be re-labelled corporate social irresponsibility.

The Economist, 30 November 2002 (p.59)

CHAPTER 17

DIRECT MARKETING

◇ Key words and concepts

direct marketing
promotional benefits
target consumers
direct mail
telemarketing
direct response advertising
catalogue marketing
electronic media
inserts
door-to-door leafleting
marketing database
customer retention
marketing mix inputs
customers
prospects
enquirers
lapsed customers
referrals
existing customers
a brief
market analysis
action plan
in-house
specialist agency
renewal rate
repeat purchasing rate
junk mail
face-to-face salesperson visit
body language
receiver
sender
niche
purchase
business-to-business markets
segment
purchasing behaviour
credit worthiness
updating
electronic home shopping
hackers
bogus companies
integrated communication campaign
intrusive nature
privacy

Instructions For Study

1° Turn to the **definitions** following the text *Direct Marketing*. They refer to the specialist terms printed in **bold** type in the list of **Key words and concepts**. Study them closely and pinpoint them in the text.
2° Use an **English** language dictionary to check the meanings (in context) of the other words in the list.
3° Do the exercises to test your comprehension, vocabulary and grammar skills.

Direct Marketing

Direct marketing is the distribution of products, information and promotional benefits to target consumers through interactive communication in a way that allows response to be measured. It includes direct mail, telemarketing, direct response advertising, catalogue marketing, electronic media (e.g. the internet), inserts in print media and door-to-door leafleting.

The growth in direct marketing activity has been driven by market and media fragmentation, developments in technology, the list explosion, sophisticated analytical techniques and co-ordinated marketing systems.

A marketing database is an electronic filing cabinet containing a list of names, addresses, telephones, lifestyle and transactional data. Database marketing is an interactive approach to marketing that uses individually addressable marketing media and channels to provide information, stimulate demand and stay close to the customer. Uses are to identify people who are more likely to respond to a direct mail or telemarketing campaign, to provide the basis for a long-term customer retention programme, to provide information and evaluate distributors, to select loyal customers for special treatment, to co-ordinate campaigns so that individuals receive consistent messages and to evaluate marketing mix inputs.

Managing a direct marketing campaign involves identifying and understanding the target audience, campaign objectives, making media and creative decisions, and executing and evaluating the campaign. Potential targets are competitors' customers, prospects, enquirers, lapsed customers, referrals and existing customers. Key objectives are the acquisition and retention of customers. Media decisions should take into account the benefits of integrated direct marketing campaigns. Creative decisions should be expressed in a brief which includes a statement of communication objectives, product benefits and weaknesses, target market analysis, development of the offer, communication of the message and an action plan. Execution may be in-house or through the use of a specialist agency. Short-term evaluation is through measures such as total sales, sales rate, number of enquiries, cost per sale and renewal rate. Longer-term evaluation is through repeat purchasing rates and the long-term value of customers generated by a given campaign.

The advantages of direct mail are that it allows close targeting of named individuals, elaborate personalization is possible and response can be measured. It depends upon access to accurate lists and initial costs can be much higher than advertising. Poor targeting can lead to the criticism of junk mail. Telemarketing also allows close targeting, two-way dialogue, lower costs than face-to-face salesperson visits and is less time consuming. However, it lacks the visual impact of a personal visit, body language cannot be assessed, some people object to receiving unsolicited telephone calls and, on a per-contact basis, it is more expensive than direct mail or media advertising.

Direct response advertising can reach large sections of the population and allow a swift response by both message receiver and sender. Direct response advertising campaigns are invariably linked to direct mail and/or telemarketing response mechanisms. Niche markets can sometimes be reached through specialist magazines and television channels. Catalogue marketing has become increasingly sophisticated in recent years. The trend has been to target specific market niches. It provides consumers with a convenient way of selecting products away from crowded shops and streets, and for rural areas it removes the necessity to travel long distances to shop. However, catalogues do not allow foods to be tried before purchase. In business-to-business markets they aid the salesperson's job when talking to customers and act as a perpetual sales aid when in the hands of customers. Responses to catalogues can be fed into a database marketing system to segment customers, record purchasing behaviour and monitor creditworthiness. Catalogue marketing can lower distribution costs although catalogues are expensive to produce and require regular updating.

Electronic home shopping forms include the internet and cable and satellite TV. The advantages to consumers are convenience, information provision and less hassle. The advantages to companies are lower costs, the ability to hold dialogues with individuals, audience measurement and flexibilty. Internet use is growing but customers need to be aware of hackers and bogus companies when using credit cards to purchase.

The major advantages of direct marketing come when integrated marketing communication campaigns are developed. The strengths of each media can be used to maximize overall impact.

Ethical issues concerning direct marketing are the quantity of poorly targeted direct mail, the timing and intrusive nature of telemarketing calls, the content of direct mail envelopes, and the invasion of privacy. Both the direct mail and telemarketing industries are taking steps to overcome these problems.

David Jobber, *Principles and Practice of Marketing*,
Maidenhead (U.K): McGraw-Hill Publishing Company, 1998 (pp.406–407)

◇◇ DEFINITIONS ◇◇◇

- ♦**direct marketing** acquiring and retaining customers without the use of an intermediary, including the distribution of products, information and promotional benefits to target consumers through interactive communication in a way which allows reponse to be measured
- ♦**direct mail** material sent through the postal service to the recipient's house or business address promoting a product and/or maintaining an ongoing relationship
- ♦**telemarketing** a marketing communications system whereby trained specialists use telecommunications and information technologies to conduct marketing and sales activities
- ♦**direct response advertising** advertising which solicits a direct response from the consumer by phone or coupon
- ♦**catalogue marketing** the sale of products through catalogue distribution to agents and customers, usually by mail or at stores if the catalogue marketer is a store owner
- ♦**marketing database** an electronic filing cabinet containing facts and details about an organisation's customers *viz.* names, addresses, telephone numbers, lifestyle and transactional data
- ♦**junk mail** mail which is sent to a prospect who is not a suitable target
- ♦**niche** small but profitable market segment
- ♦**segment** to classify customers or potential customers into groups of people sharing certain common characteristics
- ♦**electronic home shopping** buying items from home by means of computers and cable or satellite television.

Note the difference with *teleshopping*, which involves making purchases using a satellite TV channel, by phoning in on free lines

◇◇ EXERCISES ◇◇◇

◇ EXERCISE 1 *Comprehension*

(A) Answer these questions

1. What are the different methods or forms of direct marketing discussed in the text?
2. Why do companies maintain a marketing database?
3. What type of information can be recorded in a database?
4. What might the objectives of a marketing campaign be?
5. What are the stages in managing a direct marketing campaign?
6. How is a marketing campaign assessed?
7. What do *integrated marketing communication campaigns* consist in?
8. What criticisms are usually raised concerning the practice of direct marketing?
9. Why is marketing on the internet growing fast?
10. What might the obstacles to its expansion be?

(B) Complete the table below with information from the text. Write short sentences.

Direct Marketing

Method	Scope (= what it is or what it does)	Advantages	Disadvantages	Personal opinion

◊ EXERCISE 2 ***Vocabulary***

(A) Use the list of definitions above to select the appropriate term to fit each sentence

1. A directory is a useful source of information for building and updating a company's ....
2. Companies are increasingly using .... to foster long-term relationships with customers.
3. Good market research ultimately establishes whether there is a .... for the investor.
4. Another name for .... is direct response television.
5. Maintaining an up-to-date mailing list is a key factor in the success of a .... campaign.
6. People are usually annoyed when they receive .... in their letter box.
7. An advantage of .... to consumers is that it allows them to select products in the comfort of their home.
8. The difference between .... and standard advertising lies in the fact that it is designed to trigger a direct response from the prospective customer such as an order inquiry or a request for a visit.
9. .... can be inbound, when a prospective customer or prospect contacts the company by telephone or outbound, when the company is calling the prospect.
10. It is possible to .... customers in order to satisfy their requirements more effectively.

(B) Match with their meanings the following words and expressions used in the text. They refer to different **types of customer.**

competitors' customers, enquirers, existing customers,
lapsed customers, prospects, referrals, existing customers

1. people who are currently buying your products ....
2. individuals or organisations who are potential buyers of your products ....
3. people who have contacted your organisation and shown interest in your products but who have yet to buy them ....
4. people who have been recommended to your company as possible customers ......
5. people who used to buy your products but who have apparently stopped buying them ....
6. all people who buy products similar to yours sold by your competitors ....

◇ EXERCISE 3 *Grammar*

Nominal compounds

Nominal compounds are fixed expressions which are made of more than one word and which function as a word or concept.

(A) Find five examples in the text of nominal compounds with:

1. two words
2. three words
3. four words

(B) Match each noun in the left column with the appropriate one from the right to make an acceptable nominal compound

1. telephone	centre
2. inventory	channel
3. shopping	coupon
4. distribution	magazine
5. product	image
6. purchasing	segment
7. response	number
8. brand	specifications
9. market	system
10. video	behaviour

(C) Match the definitions in the left column with the appropriate three or four word nominal compounds from the right

1. a team of salespeople trained to receive phone calls and take either orders or requests for samples	a) market research results
2. a number you can ring free of charge	b) marketing information system
3. a cycle of four stages (introduction, growth, maturity and decline) in the life of a product	c) customer loyalty programmes
4. a team of salespeople trained to follow up prospects on the phone	d) distribution channel research
5. a system in which information on marketing is processed	e) freefone telephone number
6. the stages a consumer goes through when buying something	f) inbound telemarketing team
7. a colour catalogue full of products (and prices) sent to customers through the post	g) consumer decision-making process
8. the findings of research on markets	h) outbound telemarketing team
9. research aimed at locating distribution centres, dealers and agents	i) product life cycle
10. schemes in which customers are offered discounts and vouchers to encourage them to come back	j) mail order catalogue

◇ EXERCISE 4 ***Discussion***

Monitor your incoming telephone calls, e-mail messages as well as your letter box over a week and report to the class orally on any form of direct marketing you discover.

THE MARKETING MIX

◇ Key words and concepts

the marketing mix
marketplace
product
price
place
promotion
blended
time-scale
strategic elements
tactical elements
business environment
pricing
marketing plan
operational elements
advertising copy

Instructions For Study

1° Turn to the **definitions** following the text *The Marketing Mix*. They refer to the specialist terms printed in **bold** type in the list of **key words and concepts**. Study them closely and pinpoint them in the text.
2° Use an **English** language dictionary to check the meanings (in context) of the other words in the list.
3° Do the exercises to test your comprehension, vocabulary and grammar skills.

The Marketing Mix

By splitting the marketplace and developing strategies to position products, any organisation can choose an appropriate marketing mix for each target segment. The marketing mix comprises a complex set of variables which an organisation combines in order to ensure that objectives are achieved. It includes strategic, tactical and operational elements and techniques.

The concept is usually analysed on the basis of the four Ps: product, price, place and promotion. To meet customer needs an organisation must develop products to satisfy them, charge them the right price, get the goods to the right place and make the existence of the product known through its promotion.

'Mix' is an appropriate word to describe the market process. A mix is a composition of ingredients blended together to fulfill a common purpose. Every ingredient is vitally important and each depends on the contributions of the others. Just as with a cake, each ingredient is not sufficient on its own – but blended together it is possible to produce something very special. In the same way that there are a variety of cakes to suit various tastes, a marketing mix can be designed to suit the precise requirements of the market.

The marketing mix must have a time-scale. An organisation must have a plan that indicates when it expects to achieve its objectives. Some objectives will be set to be attained in the near future. Others might be medium-term (one to five years), and yet others might be visionary objectives for attainment in the longer term.

The mix must have strategic elements. These will involve the overall strategy of the organisation. They require considerable use of judgement and expertise and are only made by senior managers. Such decisions might involve the development of a new product or a new market strategy.

The mix must also have tactical or medium-term elements. The business environment has to be constantly monitored and decisions have to be taken according to whatever changes take place. External events might affect pricing strategies, product modifications or amendments to marketing plans.

There must also be short-term operational elements. These involve predictable everyday matters such as contacts with customers, analysis of advertising copy and minor decisions about packaging. The commitment and support of a programme of planning with sufficient resources will underlie the manipulation of the marketing mix and will ultimately determine how capable an organisation is of achieving its objectives.

Dave Needham & Robert Dransfield, *Advanced Business*, Oxford: Heinemann, 1995 (pp.216–217)

◇◇ DEFINITIONS ◇◇◇

- ♦**the marketing mix** framework consisting of four variables: *product, price, place, promotion*, which an organisation combines in order to ensure that objectives are achieved; *the 4Ps of marketing* or simply *the 4Ps*
- ♦**product** good or service an organisation offers or performs in order to satisfy customer needs
- ♦**price** value placed on or amount of money paid for a good or service *but also* the pricing policies of the organisation
- ♦**place** the distribution channels used, outlet locations, methods of transportation
- ♦**promotion** strategy of communication used to make the product or service known to consumers, *viz.* advertising, public relations, personal selling
- ♦**strategic elements** long-term decisions and plans made by directors setting the course the organisation must follow.
- ♦**tactical elements** flexible and medium-term actions taken by managers to implement company strategies
- ♦**business environment** the influence the wider economic situation, the customers, the suppliers and the competitors have on the performance of the organisation
- ♦**marketing plan** intended course of marketing action
- ♦**operational element** short term or immediate actions taken by managers and supervisors for the smooth running of day-to-day matters
- ♦**advertising copy** material used for making a product or service known to consumers

◇◇ EXERCISES ◇◇◇

◇ EXERCISE 1 *Comprehension*

Circle the alternative (a), (b) or (c) that most fully and correctly completes the statements or answers the questions below

1. Costs regarding advertising and the recruitment of salespeople have to be included in the decisions on
   (a) price (b) product (c) promotion

2. The product your company offers is slowly getting out of date because of technological change. The decision to find a replacement for it is
   (a) strategic (b) tactical (c) operational

3. Choices regarding brand names, warranties, packaging and services have to be considered while making decisions on
   (a) promotion (b) product (c) place

4. Which element of the marketing mix represents the profit to be made on a marketing campaign?
   (a) product (b) promotion (c) price

5. Your company wants to reach a wide market in developing countries. This objective has to be included in the budget for
   (a) place (b) promotion (c) product

6. In a supermarket, the decision to offer a free bottle of wine to customers buying a full crate is
   (a) strategic (b) tactical (c) operational

7. Which component of the marketing mix deals with the objective of making sure the products and services are available in proper quantities and qualities at the right time?
   (a) place (b) price (c) product

8. The four elements of the marketing mix should be blended means that they should be considered
   (a) separately (b) as a package (c) one by one

9. Visionary marketing objectives are goals your company intends to achieve
   (a) in the near future (b) in the short term (c) in the long run

10. Your company wants its brands to be leaders on the market in the next five years. What type of marketing objective is it?
   (a) short-term (b) medium-term (c) long term

◇ EXERCISE 2 *Vocabulary*

Use the list of definitions above to select the appropriate term to fit each sentence

1. Finding good intermediaries such as wholesalers and sales agents is a decision to be considered in the .... element of the marketing mix.
2. Like assets, elements of .... can be tangible such as posters and leaflets or intangible such as the courtesy of staff or good customer care.
3. A .... of the marketing mix could be creating an image of or even an aura around a product or brand.
4. Critics argue that the .... should additionally include process, people and physical evidence to account for services.
5. Packaging increases the appeal of a ....
6. .... of the marketing mix include decisions store managers make in order to improve sales.
7. Recent developments in air transport have compelled many airlines to modify their ....
8. Because of stiff competition amongst producers, ... seems to be an important element in the customer's choice.
9. Gathering information on competitors' prices would be a .... of the marketing mix.
10. The performance of an organisation is somewhat dependent on the ....

◇ EXERCISE 3 *Grammar*

Past tenses

(A) Underline all the verbs and modals used in the text
(B) Put these verbs and modals in the past and discuss the effect the change in tense has had on the meaning.

◇ EXERCISE 4 *Assignment*

Case Study

Visit the web site of a company you have heard about. Report to the class on the information you discover concerning the company's marketing mix.
Your account should address the following questions:

1. What product(s) does the company make or what service(s) does it provide?
2. What image does each product or service project?
3. What image does the company itself project?
4. How does the price of the product or service compare in the market? Is it the same everywhere or does it vary from one area to another? Give details if possible
5. Does the company offer discounts in some transactions?
6. How and where is each product or service advertised?
7. What distribution channels are being used for the product(s)?
8. Where are the points of sale? Are they easily accessible to customers?
9. What is your own opinion about the marketing mix of the company?

CHAPTER 18

INVENTORY MANAGEMENT

◇ Key words and concepts

inventory management
inventories
stocks
raw materials
work-in-progress
finished goods
patron
rush order
assets
dead weight
tie up
scheduling
kaizen
bottleneck
dependent inventory control
defects
retailer
jobbing manufacturer
customer demands
random
independent inventory control
inventory holding system
warehouse
control system
monitor
inputs
outputs
decision rules
supplies
fixed quantity procedure
replenishments
standard batches
cartons
containers
train loads
fixed order quantity
reorder level
delivery lead time
stock-out
accuracy

Instructions For Study

1° Turn to the **definitions** following the text *Inventory Management*. They refer to the specialist terms printed in **bold** type in the list of **Key words and concepts**. Study them closely and pinpoint them in the text.
2° Use an **English** language dictionary to check the meanings (in context) of the other words in the list
3° Do the exercises to test your comprehension, vocabulary and grammar skills.

Inventory Management

Inventories, or stocks, are the goods that the organisation transforms in the production process. Usually there are three types: raw materials, work-in-progress and finished goods.

Raw materials are the physical resources that are to form the product after processing. Examples include the metal, timber, stone and paint of the construction firm or the meat, bread and drink of the bistro.

Work-in-progress is the collection of items moving through the production process, being sometimes worked upon but commonly idle, waiting for the next stage. Partly constructed buildings and half-cooked meals are the WIP of the civil engineer and the restaurant.

Finished goods are products whose manufacture is complete but have yet to be sold. For instance, builders have to have a stock of unsold houses and, for the bistro *patron*, the display of quick snacks becomes a headache if it remains unsold.

Inventory management is a tricky task. On the one hand we must recognise that inventories are important to the functioning of many organisations. Shops must have stock to sell. Manufacturers need supplies to satisfy that rush order.

Inventory is conventionally seen as contributing to the assets of a firm – the more stock, the greater the firm's worth. On the other hand, progressive firms increasingly see stock as dead weight. It ties up capital that could be more usefully put to work elsewhere. The art is to carry enough stock to meet manufacturing and customer service targets, such as 99 per cent service levels, but to carry no more.

High inventory levels hide many problems in scheduling. The Japanese *kaizen*, continuous improvement, is applicable here. The approach is to make small reductions in stock levels and solve the problems that emerge. These could range from poor forecasting to poor quality and maintenance at a bottleneck stage. This incremental approach must take place within an inventory management strategy that sets out the way levels are to be maintained and regulated. We have what is known as *dependent inventory control*. Here, in principle, there is no stock that is not needed for orders. Excess above the minimum only arises from defects in scheduling or manufacturing processes.

Many businesses operate stocks under greater uncertainty. These range from the retailer to the jobbing manufacturer. They each seek to respond to customer demands within a shorter time than it takes to obtain raw materials. Since demand is random, these firms carry stocks unrelated to orders. Hence the control is known as *independent inventory control*. We can imagine an inventory holding system, such as a warehouse or the shelves in the book shop, together with a control system. The latter monitors inputs and outputs and uses decision rules to obtain more supplies when needed. There are many such rules, depending on circumstances. One is the fixed quantity procedure. Fixed quantities of replenishments are used when it is economic to order in standard batches. These may be cartons, containers, or train loads. The procedure works as follows:

– the inventory is replenished from time-to-time with the *fixed order quantity*;

– replenishment occurs at irregular intervals given that demand is irregular;

– new orders are placed when inventory falls to the *reorder level*;

– delivery of the orders follows a delay called the *delivery lead time*.

The reorder level is high enough to limit the risk of there being a stock-out before delivery but not so high as to make stock levels excessive. Several formulae are available to calculate order quantities and reorder points within the different control procedures. These are based on cost data whose accuracy is difficult to justify and should only be used as starting points. Improvements are made in the light of experience under the *kaizen* philosophy.

John Naylor, ***Management***,
London: Financial Times/Pitman Publishing, 1999 (pp.661-663)

◇◇ DEFINITIONS ◇◇◇

- **inventory management** continuous monitoring of stock levels an organization holds through regular checks and sales forecasts in order to influence purchase and production plans
- **stocks** goods that an organization transforms in the production process; *inventories*
- **raw materials** physical resources used as ingredients to make a product
- **work in progress (WIP)** semi or half-finished items to be used in the next production stage
- **finished goods** products whose manufacture is complete but which are waiting to be sold
- **kaizen** Japanese word for *continuous improvement*. It refers to a management philosophy in which improvement is gained by slow and steady change, and once achieved is maintained at that level until the next improvement step takes place
- **dependent inventory control** inventory monitoring method based on known or regular customer orders
- **independent inventory control** inventory monitoring method based on unknown or random customer orders
- **inventory holding system** facilities used for keeping stocks, such as a warehouse
- **delivery lead time** the time needed to deliver an order

◇◇ EXERCISES ◇◇◇

◇ EXERCISE 1 *Comprehension*

Answer these questions

1. What different types of inventory are there in the production process?
2. What is paradoxical in the holding of stocks by companies?
3. How can you make use of the *kaizen* philosphy in inventory management?
4. How many types of inventory control systems are there? Explain the differences between them
5. What does fixed quantity procedure mean in inventory management and how does it work?
6. What should a good reorder level be?
7. How is the reorder level calculated?
8. What limitations are there with these measurements?

◇ EXERCISE 2 *Vocabulary*

(A) Find in the text the occupations or activities defined in the sentences below

1. someone specializing in the planning and building of things not used for worship or war such as roads, bridges and public buildings ....

2. people who make houses ....
3. Someone who is either the manager of a public bar or a regular customer of a particular public bar ....
4. Company that produces goods in large numbers especially in a factory using machines ....
5. Someone or a company involved in selling items in small units directly to the ultimate consumer ....
6. Company producing parts or components for another mass producer ....

(B) Which problem or **situation** is being described in the following sentences. Find the appropriate phrase in the text

1. a customer needs goods urgently ....
2. the materials are not moving smoothly at this stage of production as there are too many of them flowing at the same time ....
3. you have not enough stock to meet customer demands ....
4. faults or problems in the quality of products making them unsuitable for delivery or sale ....
5. stock is a burden for your company in so far as it remains unsold ....
6. holding stock does not generate money ....

(C) Which expressions in the text are **opposites** to the following ones

1. finished goods ....
2. independent inventory control ....
3. outputs ....
4. order ....
5. replenishment ....

◇ EXERCISE 3 *Grammar*

Phrasal verbs

(A) Match the following phrasal verbs with their meanings

tie back, tie down, tie in, tie up

1. use for one purpose and not for anything else ....
2. agree with or closely conneted to ....
3. fasten someone or something in a particular position ....
4. fasten something that usually hangs down so that it is fixed in position and not hanging down ....

(B) Complete the sentences below with the appropiate phrasal verb defined above

1. *Kaizen* philosophy .... with current production methods such as *Kanban* or *Just in Time*.

2. Many people have a lot of money but most of it is .... in property.
3. Female factory workers usually .... their hair .... while doing dirty tasks.
4. Young people enjoy changing jobs partly to gain more experience and partly because they refuse to be .... by a relationship with a single employer.

◇ EXERCISE 4 ***Discussion***

Your marketing manager wants to keep large stocks in order to satify various customer demands instantly but your cost controller thinks that it is too expensive to keep large inventories.
What would you do?

ACCOUNT MANAGEMENT

◇ Key words and concepts

account management
credit
terms of payment
tied up
bills
bad debt
statements
account reminders
credit periods
credit limit
risk assessment
corporate customers
Companies House
credit-rating agency
creditworthiness
ratios
credit position
references
credit clearance
credit control
marginal customers
reliability
sales orders
debtor
monitoring accounts
overdue
sales force
administrative staff
salespeople
due payments

Instructions For Study

1° Turn to the **definitions** following the text *Account Management*. They refer to the specialist terms printed in **bold** type in the list of **Key words and concepts**. Study them closely and pinpoint them in the text.
2° Use an English language dictionary to check the meanings (in context) of the other words in the list.
3° Do the exercises to test your comprehension, vocabulary and grammar skills.

Account Management

Providing credit for customers is an important service, but is one which needs to be carefully managed within certain guidelines. On the one hand, the seller will wish to collect payment as soon as possible, but the terms of payment must also be acceptable to customers who may find better terms available elsewhere. There are a number of dangers in providing large amounts of credit.

For example, when credit is provided, money is tied up in customer accounts. It may be difficult to collect this money quickly. Credit helps to provide finance for the business of the customer. If the customer's business encounters problems which mean that they cannot pay their bills, this will lead to a bad debt.

A lot of time may be spent in account management, for example keeping and maintaining customer records and preparing statements and account reminders. At some stage the provision of credit may lead to a dispute with a customer over the amount of credit, credit periods, etc. and this may affect the selling process.

It is usual to place a credit limit on the account of each customer. These limits will normally depend upon some form of risk assessment. For new corporate customers it may be possible to go to Companies House and obtain statements. These can then be used to assess a company's financial position, but the process may take a lot of time. Another approach may be to contact a credit-rating agency for an assessment of the creditworthiness of a customer. These agencies may provide a same day analysis by computer, analyse the ratios of the business concerned or comment upon the credit position and financial position of the customer concerned.

In some situations it may be possible to ask for references on the creditworthiness of customers and to provide some form of credit clearance. After credit limits have been set for a customer, they may be subject to occasional rises as business contacts and relationships improve.

Credit control is an important part of the role of an organisation. In an ideal world customers would pay promptly, not demand long periods of credit and still be good customers for many years in the future. However, this is not always the case. Organisations may have 'marginal' customers whose reliability and ability to pay debts is not clear-cut. When sales orders are taken, the setting of credit clearance limits and the time allocated to the customer to pay should be judged carefully. Then, if customers exceed the time allocated to pay, they should be reminded about the need for prompt payment. Some systems allocate four categories of debtor – strong, average, marginal and weak. Different terms and conditions are then offered to each category.

After the transaction has taken place the credit control section will keep up to date with credit accounts and identify where accounts become overdue. There can be a danger of conflict between the sales force and the administrative staff. For example, salespeople in the field may want to concentrate simply upon the process of selling, but they have to take into account whether the customer base they create can provide payment for the purchases they make. This may often involve them in monitoring the accounts of their customers and advising them of due payments from time to time.

Dave Needham & Robert Dransfield, *Advanced Business*, Oxford: Heinemann, 1995 (pp.294–295)

◇◇ DEFINITIONS ◇◇◇

- ♦ **account management** management of costs, cash and margins
- ♦ **credit** method of deferring payment for goods or services usually including interest on top of the original amount of money
- ♦ **terms of payment** conditions under which credit is granted and the way in which it is to be honoured
- ♦ **risk assessment** evaluation of customers' credit and financial positions in order to establish their reliability and their ability to pay debts
- ♦ **credit-rating agency** firm which assesses the financial situation of companies and individuals in terms of their credit risk.
- ♦ **creditworthiness** reliability of a company and its ability to pay debts.
- ♦ **ratio** relationship between a company's assets and its liabilities aimed at establishing credit limits; *debt-equity ratio*
- ♦ **reference** testimony of the reliability and trustworthiness of a customer; *trade reference, bank reference*
- ♦ **credit control** account management activity dealing with customer monitoring, credit limits and payments
- ♦ **debtor** person or firm owing money to another person or firm

◇◇ EXERCISES ◇◇◇

◇ EXERCISE 1 *Comprehension*

Answer these questions

1. What is a bad debt?
2. What is the role of credit?
3. Can you give examples of activities involved in customer account management?
4. Why is it necessary for organisations to carry out a risk assessment before granting credit?
5. How can organisations find out about the creditworthiness of new corporate customers?
6. How many categories of debtor are found in a number of credit rating systems? What do you understand by each category?
7. What role does the credit control department of an organisation play once credit is provided?

◇ EXERCISE 2 *Vocabulary*

Use the list of definitions above to **select the appropriate term** to fit each sentence

1. Companies selling goods or providing services to others often do so on .... as opposed to cash.
2. A business may impose penalty clauses as part of the ....

3. Large firms have .... departments which use letters and phone calls to remind customers about payment and which sometimes take legal action.
4. Before providing credit, a firm could make enquiries with a .... to see if the firm concerned has a clean record of trustworthiness.
5. If you wish to keep an eye on a ...., you have to invoice them quickly and correctly.
6. The standard practice in many countries of the world is not to grant credit to companies exceeding a 1:1 ....
7. Before granting credit, a firm will usually ask for a .... from a bank or a supplier who has previously given credit to the business concerned.
8. Many businesses have been brought down by organisations which had failed to pay their bills before vanishing. It is therefore necessary to assess the .... of the customers you are dealing with.
9. Institutional investors always carry out a .... of their prospective customers.
10. Credit control, risk assessment and invoicing are all activities in involved in customer ....

◇ EXERCISE 3 *Grammar*

Modals

(A) **Underline** all the modals used in the text

(B) **Complete** the following sentences, with a suitable modal used in the text.

1. Customers who save every month .... get a much higher return on their savings.
2. Insurance companies .... never refuse you cover because of your age.
3. When using travellers cheques and foreign currency, you .... have to pay commissions and conversion charges.
4. It is commonly believed that top managers .... be rewarded for the way they manage their organisations.
5. With your visa card, you .... withdraw cash from cash dispensers anywhere in the world.

PART F

LAW

IN THIS PART YOU WILL READ ABOUT

- Roman Law systems and common law systems
- Legal rights and liberties
- The sources of English law
- Civil cases and criminal cases
- Double jeopardy and hearsay evidence
- Miscarriage of justice
- The different branches of the legal profession in England and Wales
- The scales of justice
- The workings of the court system and the legal profession in the USA
- Mass torts
- State aid to religious schools

YOU WILL LEARN SOME BASIC LEGAL TERMS CONCERNING

- Civil law and common law
- Statute law
- Crimes and torts
- Solicitors and barristers
- Courts, lawyers and litigation in the USA

CHAPTER 19

TWO KINDS OF LAW

◇ Key words and concepts

civil law
disputes
sue
praetor
summon
lawyer
advice
worked out
rule upon
codified
scholars
relevance
judges
drew on
underlie
brand

common law
mainstream
subdued
owes
inquire into
civil cases
criminal cases
bit by bit
arose
enjoy
former
rights
duties
remedies
damages
raw material

Instructions For Study

1° Turn to the **definitions** following the text *Two Kinds of Law*. They refer to the specialist terms printed in **bold** type in the list of **Key words and concepts**. Study them closely and pinpoint them in the text.
2° Use an **English** language dictionary to check the meanings (in context) of the other words in the list.
3° Do the exercises to test your comprehension, vocabulary and grammar skills.

Two Kinds of Law

The first great legal system of the western world was **civil law**–the law of Rome, the law applying to the Roman citizen (*civis Romanus*). The most important part of this law was concerned with private disputes. Suppose Brutus stole some of Caesar's marble and used it to make a statue. Caesar might sue Brutus before the **praetor**. This government minister would summon a jury to decide if Caesar's story were true. However, the praetor was not a lawyer but a politician (and usually a soldier), so would seek advice from experts. In Rome the experts were law professors who discussed both real and hypothetical cases, and worked out what the law would say about them. Though the praetors ruled upon the law, we can say that Roman law was basically created by professors.

Roman law had a long history. It served a city that was founded in 753 B.C., acquired an enormous empire and lasted until the fourteenth century A.D., Though Rome itself fell in the fifth century, the eastern empire, ruled from Constantinople, remained. Roman law was **codified** in A.D. 529, so it endured for well over a thousand years.

After the fall of Rome, Europe became divided into many countries with regions each with its own laws, so Roman law was no longer applied. Its influence resurfaced with the foundation of mediaeval universities in the twelfth century in Europe. Bologna in Italy, Paris in France and soon afterwards Oxford in England were the first of these. Scholars came from all over Europe to study a variety of subjects, but none was more significant than law.

The mediaeval universities didn't teach the law of Bologna, Paris or Oxford. Something of wider relevance was wanted by the scholars who would later be judges and administrators in their countries. Instead of teaching local law the professors taught the students the law as worked out by the professors themselves on the basis of three things: common sense, Christian doctrine and Roman law that along with other ancient literature was then being rediscovered. Law teachers drew heavily on Roman law answers to legal problems, as did their students when developing the law in their own countries. Later, as France and other European countries began to systemize and codify their laws, the codes were based on Roman law. So with one exception the civil law of Rome came to underlie all legal thinking and development in Europe.

England as a whole never fell under the influence of Roman law, never received Roman law and never produced a code based on Roman law. Instead it developed its own particular brand of law–the common law.

There are two reasons why England developed its own law. As an island, England was isolated from the mainstream of European development. And because of its small size, it was easily subdued and unified under one government. Historically, common law owes its existence to the fact that the Norman monarchs who ruled England for the first century or two after the Norman conquest in 1066 were the most powerful and dynamic line of rulers in Europe. To extend their power over the whole country they sent royal judges out to every part of it to inquire into its administration and to hear civil and criminal cases. Bit by bit, dispensing royal justice and dealing with each problem as it arose, they looked for guidance – not to the teachings of professors, but to judicial practice and precedent (i.e. previous decisions). These judges fashioned a general law common to the whole of England as contrasted with the local laws in force only in local areas.

Common law grew in power and in prestige. The judges creating it were powerful figures acting for the monarch. The lawyers practising in their courts developed a high degree of professionalism. Both judges and lawyers jealously guarded the common law against the influence of Roman law. Unlike the local laws on the continent, then, the common law of England proved strong enough to resist the influence of Roman law. Consequently England and the countries that were once its colonies today enjoy a law different from that of the other European countries and their former colonies.

To understand these two different approaches, let us return to the hypothetical case of the marble statue. Brutus takes a piece of Caesar's marble and uses it to make a statue, and Caesar sues him. The Roman law professors would approach the matter academically and concentrate on the abstract question of rights and duties. Who owns the statue? Brutus because he sculpted it, or Caesar because he owned the marble?

In England the law was worked out by the judges, who would usually approach the matter more practically and concentrate not on rights but on remedies. Can Caesar take possession of the statue? Can he get damages from Brutus for taking his marble? Can Brutus keep the statue? Can Brutus make Caesar pay him the difference between the value of the statue and the value of the raw material?

In short, civil law concentrates on rights, common law on remedies.

Patrick Fitzgerald & Gretchen Kewley, *This Law of Ours*,
Sydney: Prentice-Hall, 1978 (pp.35-36)

◇◇ DEFINITIONS ◇◇◇

- ♦ **civil law** (1) originally the law of ancient Rome, that is, a civil law system as against a common law one (2) the law that does not deal with criminal matters but with the enforcement of rights and obligations
- ♦ **sue** to bring a civil action against someone
- ♦ **praetor** a magistrate of ancient Rome
- ♦ **lawyer** someone who has studied law and is legally authorized to represent people in court or in other circumstances
- ♦ **rule upon** make official decisions
- ♦ **codified** when the law has been written down according to its basic principles (as in Civil law countries, e.g. France)
- ♦ **judges** the impartial arbitrators who preside over courts
- ♦ **common law** the law made by judges as they rule upon cases brought before them in court
- ♦ **civil cases** matters dealing with the enforcement of a person's rights or obligations
- ♦ **criminal cases** matters dealing with wrongs (acts harmful to the state or its citizens) for which a person can be punished
- ♦ **rights** protections, freedoms or guarantees provided by the state
- ♦ **duties** obligations upon an individual to do something
- ♦ **remedies** the legal solutions to matters brought before the court by plaintiffs
- ♦ **damages** compensation in the form of money that the court orders one party to pay another
- ♦ **raw material** a natural substance (e.g. marble) used to make something (e.g. a statue)

◇◇ EXERCISES ◇◇◇

◇ EXERCISE 1 *Comprehension*

True / False Circle the correct choice and justify your answer

1. Roman law has exerted an uninterrupted influence in Europe. T / F
2. In the Middle Ages, local law was the basis of law teaching in Europe. T / F
3. Common law was built up on the basis of judicial practice and precedent. T / F
4. The former English colonies developed a law different from that of England. T / F
5. Common law is characterized by a more pragmatic approach than civil law. T / F

◇ EXERCISE 2 *Vocabulary*

Find words or expressions in the text with equivalent terms to those in italics below

1. He would *order* a jury to be called.
2. He would *look for help*.
3. The specialists would *determine* what the law would say.

4. Roman law *lasted* for more than a thousand years.
5. Law teachers *relied a lot* on Roman law to find answers to legal problems.
6. The law of Rome *became the basis* of all legal thinking in Europe.
7. England was easily *brought under control*
8. Can Caesar *receive compensation?*

◇ EXERCISE 3 *Grammar*

Simple past and present perfect tense

(A) Complete the passage below choosing between the **simple past** or **present perfect** tense

I (*always, to think*) that injustice is really awful, probably because my school teacher (*to slap*) me once, when I (*to be*) eight. I (*never, to forget*) it, because it (*to be*) so unfair. I (*to have*) a great respect for authority in those days, and like all children, I (*to think*) that teachers (*never, to make*) mistakes. Needless to say, I (*to change one's mind*) since then. After all, I (*to make*) hundreds of mistakes myself, over the years !

(B) Make sentences **contrasting** the evolution of the legal system in England and the legal system in continental Europe using *unlike, whereas, contrary to*

FUNDAMENTAL RIGHTS

◇ Key words and concepts

contracts
trespass
damages
wrongs
rights
common law
tort
lawful
interfere
sue
prosecute
remedy
wrongdoers
rule of law

Instructions For Study

1° Turn to the **definitions** following the text *Fundamental Rights*. They refer to the specialist terms printed in **bold** type in the list of **Key words and concepts.** Study them closely and pinpoint them in the text.
2° Use an **English** language dictionary to check the meanings (in context) of the other words in the list.
3° Do the exercises to test your comprehension, vocabulary and grammar skills.

Fundamental Rights

Which part of the law says what can be done?

Curiously, no special part of law does this. No laws say we can eat, drink and be merry. Our law doesn's work like that; it says only that we can't do various things–that if we murder or steal we'll be punished, if we break our contracts or trespass on other people's property we'll have to pay damages. Ours is a law of wrongs, not a law of rights. So how do we come to have any legal rights and liberties?

First, we have legal rights by implication, an implication that is at the heart of the common law on which Australian law is based. That law, as we saw, developed bit by bit as the English judges held this, that or the other to be a crime, a tort or some other kind of legal wrong. Meanwhile, anything not held to be a legal wrong remained lawful and allowable. If there's no law against it, then it can be done–that was and still is the basic principle of common law. This means that if there's no law against something, we don't need a law for it. We don't need a law telling us we can do it, for we know this already simply because the law doesn't say we can't. Our law, then, is a set of restrictions on individuals otherwise left fundamentally free.

One thing we're not left free to do is to interfere with the freedom of others. I am free to eat and drink but not to stop you doing the same. If I do so by force you can sue or prosecute me for assault. Here lies the second source of all our legal liberties–the fact that whenever one person does interfere with the rights and liberties of another, that other has a remedy in law. "Where there's a right there's a remedy", runs the legal maxim; and the common law, a practical law for practical people, was always far more interested in the remedy than in the right itself. By stressing not rights but wrongs and the remedies for them, the common law achieved two things: it left people a residue of freedom and gave the individual protection against all enemies of that freedom–with one exception.

The exception, though unimportant now, was once far more important than the rule itself. It concerned threats to liberty posed not by ordinary wrongdoers, but by someone far more dangerous–the monarch. In early times, just as in modern ones, the greatest threat to liberty came from the government itself. In early times, if there was one person people needed protection from, it was the monarch. Yet the monarch was the person common law gave no remedies against.

The reason was, of course, that the common law was the law developed by the monarch's own judges. Naturally enough they held that in law their monarch could do no wrong. Things that were legally wrong when done by ordinary people were not legally wrong when done by the monarch–who could seize you, arrest you and lock you up. You were legally powerless, for no one could sue or prosecute the monarch. Here law had reached its limit, its end; and, as Prime Minister Pitt observed in 1770, "Where law ends tyranny begins."

Fortunately, however, the monarchy was transformed, though slowly, into a constitutional monarchy. Arbitrary power gave way to the rule of law, and the judges solved the problem posed by the rule that the monarch could do no legal wrong. Indeed they turned this weakness of the law to the advantage of the citizen.

Patrick Fitzgerald & Gretchen Kewley, *This Law of Ours*,
Sydney: Prentice-Hall, 1978 (pp.150-151)

◇◇ DEFINITIONS ◇◇◇

♦ **contract** a legally binding agreement between two or more parties
♦ **trespass** to enter someone's property without their permission
♦ **damages** compensation in the form of money that the court orders one party to pay another
♦ **wrongs** acts that cause injury to others and for which compensation (damages) can be claimed in civil proceedings; *torts*
♦ **rights** protections, freedoms or guarantees provided by the state
♦ **common law** the law made by judges as they rule upon cases brought before them in court
♦ **tort** any civil wrong for which the injured party may sue for damages (e.g. negligence); *wrong*
♦ **lawful** allowed by law, acceptable to the law
♦ **sue** to bring a civil action against someone
♦ **prosecute** to bring criminal proceedings against an accused person
♦ **remedy** the legal solution to a matter brought before the court by a plaintiff
♦ **rule of law** the notion that people will be treated fairly by the state and that no-one is above the law

◇◇ EXERCISES ◇◇◇

◇ EXERCISE 1 *Comprehension*

True / False Circle the correct choice and justify your answer

1. Australian law is a law of wrongs. T / F
2. The common law basically leaves the individual free to do whatever he likes. T / F
3. The common law gave individuals protection against all restrictions of their freedom. T / F
4. The monarch's own judges put the monarch above the law. T / F
5. We are free to interfere with others if they interfere with us. T / F

◇ EXERCISE 2 *Vocabulary*

Complete each phrase with a suitable **particle** from the list below

Out / away / with / up / over / down

1. to break .... a gang
2. to draw .... a list of suspects.
3. to work .... what the law says.
4. to do .... with old laws.
5. to carry .... the law

6. to deal .... a criminal case
7. to preside .... a court
8. to cope .... a problem
9. to give .... hope
10. to make .... rules
11. to lay .... the law
12. to bring .... a ruling

◇ EXERCISE 3 *Grammar*

Determiners

Supply the **missing articles** where necessary

Trial by Jury

In Australia ....(1) Magistrates' Courts also conduct ....(2) preliminary hearings, also called ....(3) committal proceedings, when ....(4) serious (indictable) offences are charged. ....(5) indictable offence is ....(6) crime that must be tried by ....(7) jury. If ....(8) Magistrates' Court is satisfied that there is enough evidence on which ....(9) person charged with ....(10) indictable offence might be found guilty, then ....(11) offender is committed for trial before ....(12) judge and ....(13) jury in either ....(14) County Court or ....(15) Supreme Court. If ....(16) evidence is insufficient, then ....(17) charge is dismissed there and then.

FROM THE NEWS

CIVIL LIBERTIES

British changes rules to cut crime

◇ EXERCISE

Read the article below and discuss or write answers to the following questions

1. Why is the government acting?
2. Where does public opinion stand?
3. What is being done to the double-jeopardy rule?
4. Does everyone agree with these changes?
5. What fundamental issue is at stake here?

British change rules to cut crime

LONDON: Britain has announced sweeping changes in its criminal justice system, scrapping the ancient double-jeopardy rule that prevents people from being tried twice for the same crime, making hearsay evidence admissible in court and letting jurors know of suspects' previous crimes.

The plan also introduces trial without jury in serious fraud cases where there is a risk of jury intimidation, allows the police to lock up dangerous sexual or violent offenders indefinitely and adjusts sentencing guidelines to tailor the punishment to the criminal, not just the crime.

With crime levels soaring and public confidence in the police and the courts plunging, Home Secretary David Blunkett told the House of Commons on Wednesday that the time had come to "rebalance the criminal justice system in favor of the victim and bring justice to all."

Crime is a big political issue in Britain. Last week, government figures showed street crime had risen 28 percent in the year ending in April. Prime Minister Tony Blair came into office in 1997 saying he would concentrate as much on the causes of crime as on crime itself, but has shifted his emphasis as a result of the increasing violence and the growing public impression that the legal process rewards the guilty because of inadequate police work and skillful defense lawyers.

A government report last month pointed to the gulf between the number of crimes reported – 5.2 million in the past year – and the number of criminals sentenced in the same period – 326,000.

Public opinion has also been stirred by two high-profile cases in which sloppy police work led to widely condemned acquittals: the 1993 killing of a black teenager, Stephen Lawrence, by white toughs, and the death of a 10-year-old Nigerian immigrant, Damilola Taylor, in November 2000.

Blunkett has made it clear since becoming home secretary last year that he would apply his hard-line views to the problem, and both his political stature and popularity have grown as a result.

He said on Wednesday that the removal of the double-jeopardy rule would be adopted only in serious cases like murder, rape, manslaughter and armed robbery. He told the lawmakers that advances in DNA and forensic science meant that "compelling new evidence" calling into question not-guilty verdicts now arises more frequently. The change would be retrospective, and in cases where it was applied, the Court of Appeal would be asked to quash the earlier acquittal.

As for the sentencing changes, Blunkett cited a case last year in which a sex offender considered still dangerous was released because the government "had no power whatsoever" to keep him inside. After he was freed, he kidnapped and sexually assaulted a young woman, Blunkett said.

Police groups welcomed the announcement Wednesday. Fred Broughton, chairman of the Police Federation of England and Wales – the two parts of Britain where the reforms will be carried out – said: "For years, the criminal justice system has been failing victims, with the odds heavily stacked in favor of the accused. The police federation wants to see a trial system based on a search for the truth rather than the game that currently exists."

But John Wadham, director of Liberty, a civil liberties group, questioned both the changes and the motivation behind them.

"Politicians feel they must look tough at all costs, but the cost here is that crime levels will go untouched, while British justice will be seriously damaged," he said. "Eroding the rights of suspects won't give victims the rights they have waited too long to receive."

CHAPTER 20

ENGLISH LAW TODAY

◇ Key words and concepts

common law
statute law
rules
cases
judgements
judges
precedents
deduce
underlying
House of Lords
rulings
current
consistency
fail to
Acts of Parliament
bill
Royal Assent
Privy Council
penalties
damages
civil law
take precedence over
domestic

Instructions For Study

1° Turn to the **definitions** following the text *English Law Today*. They refer to the specialist terms printed in **bold** type in the list of **Key words and concepts**. Study them closely and pinpoint them in the text.
2° Use an **English** language dictionary to check the meanings (in context) of the other words in the list.
3° Do the exercises to test your comprehension, vocabulary and grammar skills.

English Law Today

The three main sources of English law today are the common law, statute law and European Union law.

The oldest source is the *common law,* which is based on the customs of successive settlers and invaders from Europe. After the Norman Conquest, it became a uniform body of rules and principles that were decided and written down by judges in court cases (case law). These judgments were recognized as the law of the land and were applied by common law courts. Today, the same rules guide judges in their interpretation of statutes and in the expansion of the common law itself.

Common law decisions form precedents from which later judges can deduce the principles of law that may be applied to new cases. Precedents are strong in English law and the judges of the lower courts must generally follow them. Normally, the power to create new precedents is reserved to the House of Lords, as the supreme court of appeal. Its rulings represent the current state of the law to be applied by all courts. The tradition of following precedent maintains consistency and continuity. But it can also make the law conservative and fail to take account of changing social conditions.

Statute law was originally created by the monarch, but by the thirteenth century was gradually made through royal orders in response to petitions from Parliament. Parliament itself later became the legislating authority because of its growing power against the monarch. Modern statutes are a nineteenth- and twentieth-century development and arose because new rules were required to meet the needs of a rapidly changing society.

Statutes are Acts of Parliament, created after a bill has passed through Parliament. Parliament makes new laws, which have usually been initiated by the government. Acts are supreme over all other forms of law (except for some European Union law). From 2000, the Privy Council will resolve any conflicts between Westminster Acts and Scottish Parliament Acts. Much British law (criminal and civil) is now in statute form and shows the influence of the state in citizens' lives.

European Union law became part of English (British) law following Britain's entry into the European Economic Community in 1973. EU law takes precedence over British domestic law in certain areas, and judges must apply EU law when there is a conflict with Acts of Parliament. EU law and British domestic law now coexist, and Britain plays its part in creating EU law.

John Oakland, *British Civilisation*, London: Routledge, 2000 (pp.152-153)

◇◇ DEFINITIONS ◇◇◇

- ♦ **common law** the law made by judges as they rule upon cases brought before them in court; *case law*
- ♦ **statute law** all law made by parliament
- ♦ **rules** a set of guidelines that govern a particular activity or process
- ♦ **cases** matters that are heard before a court
- ♦ **judgements** judges' rulings on cases brought before them
- ♦ **judges** the impartial arbitrators who preside over courts
- ♦ **precedents** earlier judicial decisions on which a judge bases later rulings
- ♦ **House of Lords** the upper house of English Parliament
- ♦ **rulings** the official decisions made by judges
- ♦ **Acts of Parliament** statutes or laws passed by Parliament
- ♦ **bill** the name given to proposed legislation when it is introduced and debated in Parliament
- ♦ **Royal Assent** the signature of the Queen on statutes which signifies her agreement
- ♦ **Privy Council (the)** body of senior advisors to the Queen
- ♦ **penalties** sanctions or forms of coercion obliging a party to obey the law
- ♦ **damages** compensation in the form of money that the court orders one party to pay another
- ♦ **civil law** the law that does not deal with criminal matters but with enforcing rights and obligations

◇◇ EXERCISES ◇◇◇

◇ EXERCISE 1 *Comprehension*

Circle the alternative (a), (b) or (c) that most fully and correctly completes the statements below

1. A statute becomes law when it
   a) has been passed by the House of Lords
   b) has received Royal Assent
   c) has been through both Houses of Parliament

2. The common law
   a) was fixed once and for all by history
   b) can evolve on the basis of new judgements
   c) must be recognized by an Act of Parliament

3. Civil law
   a) takes precedence over European law
   b) mainly takes the form of statutes
   c) remains essentially part of the common law

4. The doctrine of precedent
   a) enables judges to interpret new legal situations
   b) has fixed rules which do not alter
   c) was developed by the House of Lords

5. European Union Law
   a) takes precedence over British law
   b) is created by Acts of the British Parliament
   c) must be applied in certain areas of domestic law

◇ EXERCISE 2 *Vocabulary*

Use the list of definitions above to **select the appropriate term** to fit each sentence

1. Within the .... is the division between statute law and judge-made law.
2. In the law of tort, compensation for injuries is referred to as ....
3. When you look at what previous judges have said in similar cases, you look for help from ....
4. Legislation to implement government policies when introduced into Parliament is called a ....
5. In civil .... it is not necessary that the defendant comes to court.

◇ EXERCISE 3 *Grammar*

Obligation and necessity

Choose the correct word or phrase in italics to complete each sentence

1. You *mustn't / don't have to* find the accused guilty unless you're satisfied beyond reasonable doubt that he did kill the deceased.
2. Countries wishing to join the European Union *must / needn't* do away with capital punishment.
3. EU law *hasn't got to / can't* take precedence over British domestic law in all areas.
4. When ruling upon new cases judges *don't have to / aren't allowed* to ignore precedent.
5. The jury *needn't / mustn't* stay in the courtroom to consider its verdict.

CIVIL CASES AND CRIMINAL CASES

◇ Key words and concepts

civil cases
criminal cases
prosecution
crime
burglary
offender
sues
harm
owed
run down
contract
amounts to
tort
negligence
fine
injured
compensation
conviction
balance of probabilities
plaintiff
defendant
highlighted
intruder
trespass
theft
insider dealing
computer hacking
criminal offence

Instructions For Study

1° Turn to the **definitions** following the text *Civil Cases and Criminal Cases*. They refer to the specialist terms printed in **bold** type in the list of **Key words and concepts**. Study them closely and pinpoint them in the text.
2° Use an **English** language dictionary to check the meanings (in context) of the other words in the list.
3° Do the exercises to test your comprehension, vocabulary and grammar skills.

Civil Cases and Criminal Cases

What is the difference between civil and criminal cases? In a criminal case someone is prosecuted for conduct, which we call criminal, which is considered harmful to society as a whole. There are, of course, individual victims of murder or burglary but, in a wider sense, all crimes affect us all. So, normally the prosecution is brought by the state (using the Queen's name – cases are listed as Regina v. Accused), although individuals may also bring a prosecution. If found guilty, the offender will be punished by the state.

Civil cases are between private interests. An individual (or company, local authority or some other organization) sues another, usually for some harm caused to him personally, or for money owed to him. Perhaps the person he is suing has run him down and fractured his leg, or has broken a contract. The police will not be interested unless the same behaviour also amounts to a crime. For example, a driver who knocks down a pedestrian may be guilty of the crime of dangerous or careless driving. The same accident gives the victim the right to sue the driver for the tort (legal terminology for a civil wrong) of negligence. So the driver can be prosecuted for dangerous driving in a criminal court, convicted and sent to prison or ordered to pay a fine, which goes to the state. Later he may be sued by the person he has injured, found negligent, and be ordered to pay compensation to the victim for the injury suffered. Or he may win one case and lose the other, because different things have to be proved in civil and criminal cases. The degree of proof required is also different. In criminal cases there can only be a conviction if the case has been proved 'beyond reasonable doubt' – very near certainty. A civil case is won on the less difficult test of 'balance of probabilities' – is it more likely than not?

In civil cases, the person suing was, until 1999, known as the plaintiff, but is now officially called the claimant, and the person sued is the defendant. In criminal cases, the person accused of the crime is called either the accused or the defendant.

The distinction between a crime and a civil wrong was highlighted in 1982 when an intruder broke into the Queen's bedroom at Buckingham Palace. Entering someone else's home without permission is trespass: not a crime, but a civil wrong. It only becomes a crime if the intruder uses, or threatens to use, violence, or causes damage, say by breaking a lock or a window, or if he intends to commit a crime (such as theft) once inside. Because Michael Fagan's intrusion was a simple trespass, he could not be prosecuted for that, although the incident did lead to (unsuccessful) calls for that kind of trespass to be made a crime. But a trespasser can be sued in the civil courts. (It follows that the sign 'Trespassers will be prosecuted' doesn't make sense, legally.)

New crimes are being created all the time, as society revises its thinking about the sorts of behaviour it wants to discourage. For example, insider dealing in the City only became a crime in the mid-1980s, even though the practice had been going on for many years. New technology can result in new crimes – computer hacking, for example, has been made a criminal offence.

It is a fundamental principle of English justice that what happens in the courts should be open and public. There are exceptions, such as where young children are involved, or there is a risk to national security. But, in general, English justice is open justice, and any member of the public can see what goes on in any court.

Marcel Berlins & Clare Dyer, *The Law Machine*, London: Penguin, 2000 (pp.17-19)

◇◇ DEFINITIONS ◇◇◇

♦ **civil cases** matters dealing with the enforcement of a person's rights or obligations
♦ **criminal cases** matters dealing with wrongs (acts harmful to the state or its citizens) for which a person can be punished
♦ **prosecution** when criminal proceedings are brought against an accused person
♦ **crime** an act that the state considers harmful to itself or its citizens and which is punished by law
♦ **offender** the person who has committed a crime
♦ **sue** to bring a civil action against someone
♦ **contract** a legally binding agreement between two or more parties
♦ **tort** an act that causes injury to others and for which compensation (damages) can be claimed in civil proceedings
♦ **negligence** where one party owes another a duty of care, and breaches that duty by causing harm to the other party
♦ **fine** a punishment ordered by a court in which the guilty party must pay a specific sum of money
♦ **compensation** payment for loss, injury or damages
♦ **conviction** when the defendant is declared guilty at the conclusion of a trial
♦ **balance of probabilities** the standard of proof in a civil case
♦ **plaintiff** the party bringing an action in a civil case; *claimant*
♦ **defendant** in a legal action, the person sued or the person accused of a wrong
♦ **trespass** to enter someone's property without their permission
♦ **insider dealing** buying or selling the stock of a company by persons on the basis of confidential (inside) information derived from their connection with the company or people they know in it
♦ **computer hacking** intruding into someone's personal computer files with a view to misusing the information they contain, sometimes with criminal intent
♦ **criminal offence** a crime

◇◇ EXERCISES ◇◇◇

◇ EXERCISE 1 *Comprehension*

Answer these questions

1. What is the basic difference between civil cases and criminal cases?
2. Are the police interested in civil cases?
3. Are people convicted in the same way in civil and criminal cases?
4. Why doesn't the sign 'Trespassers will be prosecuted' make sense legally?
5. Why did insider trading in the City become a crime so late?

◇ EXERCISE 2 *Vocabulary*

(A) Fill in the blanks with the words listed below

assault / tort of assault / sue / strikes / theft / proceedings / breach of contract / wrong / damages / prosecuted / committing / runs off

The same facts may lead to both criminal and civil ....(1). If your neighbour ....(2) you, you can either have him ....(3) by the police for the crime of ....(4), or ....(5) him yourself for ....(6) in a civil action for the ....(7). Again, if I ask a night porter to mind my valuables and he ....(8) with them, he is probably ....(9) the crime of ....(10) and the civil ....(11) known as ....(12).

(B) Make correct sentences by selecting the beginning in the left-hand column which **matches** the end in the right-hand one

1. The clerk of the court	(a) may be cross-examined
2. After hearing the evidence, the judge	(b) pleads guilty or not guilty
3. After giving his evidence, the witness	(c) passes sentence
4. At the start of the trial, the defendant	(d) considers its verdict
5. At the end of the trial, the judge	(e) reads out the charge against the defendant
6. When the evidence is finished, the jury	(f) sums up

◇ EXERCISE 3 *Grammar*

Modals

Complete these sentences using *may* / *must* / *have to* / *should* / *can* / *could*

1. If you want to claim damages, you ....
2. If you want to have someone prosecuted, you ....
3. If somebody is caught stealing, he ....
4. If somebody commits a crime, they ....
5. If you breach a contract, you ....
6. If someone indulges in unfair trade practices, they ....
7. If a person is run down by a car, he ....
8. If you trespass on private property, you ....

FROM THE NEWS

MISCARRIAGE OF JUSTICE

Race row killer to be breed

◇ EXERCISE

Read the article below and discuss or write answers to the following questions

1. Why did Mr Ram stab the white man?
2. Why is Mr Ram still in jail?
3. What stance has the European Court of Human Rights taken?
4. What is the difference between a victory and complete vindication?
5. How is the Pearce family reacting?

Race row killer to be freed

An Asian man who says he was wrongly convicted of murder after defending himself from a racist attack is to be released after 15 years in jail, the Home Office confirmed last week.

Friends and supporters of Satpal Ram, 36, who was jailed for life in 1987 for stabbing a white man in an Indian restaurant in Birmingham during a fight, say he is the victim of one of the worst miscarriages of justice in recent years.

Mr Ram said the man, Clarke Pearce, had racially abused him before attacking and slashing him with broken glass. The judge at his trial had recommended he serve an 11-year sentence, but Mr Ram was kept in jail longer because he refused to admit his guilt.

He is expected to be freed this week as a result of a ruling last month by the European Court of Human Rights.

In a separate case, Strasbourg judges ruled that the Home Secretary had no right to overrule a decision of a parole board to release a prisoner, known as the Stafford ruling.

This is what had happened to Mr Ram in 2000 when, in an unprecedented move, the then home secretary, Jack Straw, reversed a parole board decision to free him. The board had said Mr Ram no longer posed a danger to the public.

Last week government lawyers decided they could not oppose a court challenge to Mr Straw's decision launched by Mr Ram's lawyers.

Mr Ram's lawyer, Daniel Guedalla, said: "It does not mean they accept he is innocent and he is still challenging his wrongful conviction. This is a victory but not complete vindication. He is still on a life licence until his conviction is quashed. He lost 18 months or more of his liberty because of Jack Straw interfering."

Mr Ram has been in repeated clashes with prison authorities and has been moved more than 65 times to different prisons. He says he has been victimised by prison officers.

The prospect of Mr Ram's release was condemned by the dead man's family. Mr Pearce's sister, Jane Smith, told the Birmingham Evening Mail: "I'm disgusted. Life should mean life. He murdered my brother."

Vikram Dodd, *Guardian Weekly*,
20 June 2002 (p.13)

CHAPTER 21

THE LEGAL PROFESSION IN ENGLAND AND WALES

◇ Key words and concepts

solicitors
practise
Law Society
spectrum
partnership
conveyancing
probate
litigation
monopoly
licensed
building societies
rely upon
fees
university degree
passing
apprenticeship
trainee
training
barristers
appear
Bar
Council of Legal Education
Inns of Court
terms
self-employed
chambers
briefs
earning
drop out
practice
take silk
charge
judges
seniority
located
appointed
office
retiring age
dismissed
complaints
complaints board
removable
designed
involvement

Instructions For Study

1° Turn to the **definitions** following the text *The Legal Profession in England and Wales*. They refer to the specialist terms printed in **bold** type in the list of **Key words and concepts**. Study them closely and pinpoint them in the text.
2° Use an **English** language dictionary to check the meanings (in context) of the other words in the list.
3° Do the exercises to test your comprehension, vocabulary and grammar skills.

The Legal Profession in England and Wales

There are some 83,000 *solicitors*, who practise mainly in private firms, but also in local and central government, legal centres and industry. Most are now organized by their self-regulating professional body, the Law Society. The solicitors' branch is a middle-class profession, but it is increasingly attracting members from a relatively wide spectrum of society.

Solicitors deal with general legal work, although many now specialize in one area of the law. Their firms (or partnerships) offer services such as conveyancing (the buying and selling of property); probate (wills and succession after death); family matters; criminal and civil litigation; commercial cases; and tax and financial affairs. Conveyancing, which used to be a monopoly for solicitors, may now be done by licensed conveyancers, banks and building societies. This reform has caused difficulty for some solicitors' firms that rely upon conveyancing fees as their chief source of finance.

In order to become a solicitor, it is now necessary to have a university degree, not necessarily in law. After passing additional professional examinations organized by the Law Society, the student serves a practical apprenticeship as a trainee solicitor with an established solicitor for some two years. After this total period of about six years' education and training, the new solicitor can practise law.

There are 8,000 *barristers* (known as advocates in Scotland) in private practice, who have the right to appear before any court in England and Wales. They belong to the Bar, which is an ancient legal institution controlled by the self-regulating Bar Council and four Inns of Court in London (Gray's Inn, Lincoln's Inn, Middle Temple and the Inner Temple). Barristers have two main functions: first, to give specialized advice on legal matters, and second, to act as advocates in the courts. Most of the general public cannot approach a barrister directly, but must be introduced by a solicitor.

In order to become a barrister, one must usually have a university degree, pass professional examinations and become a member of an Inn of Court. The student must dine in the Inn for a number of terms before being 'called to the

Bar', or accepted as a barrister. He or she must then serve for a one-year period (pupillage) under a practising barrister. After this total training period of about five years, the new barrister can practise alone.

Barristers are self-employed individuals who practise the law from chambers (or offices), together with other barristers. The barrister's career starts as a 'junior' handling minor briefs (or cases). He or she may frequently have difficulty in earning a reasonable living or in becoming established in the early years of practice, with the result that many barristers drop out and enter other fields. However, should the barrister persist and build up a successful practice as a junior, he or she may then 'take silk' and become a Queen's Counsel (QC). A QC is a senior barrister who can charge higher fees for his or her work, but who is then excluded from appearing in lesser cases. Appointment as a QC may lead to a future position as a judge, and it is regarded as a necessary career step for the ambitious.

The *judges* constitute the judiciary, or independent third branch of the constitutional system. There are a relatively small number of judges at various levels of seniority, who are located in most large cities and in the higher courts in London. They are appointed from the ranks of senior barristers, although solicitors have now become eligible for some of the lower posts.

Once appointed, senior judges cannot be removed from office until the retiring age of 75, although junior judges can be dissmissed by the Lord Chancellor for good reasons before retirement age at 72. There have been proposals that complaints against judges and their possible dismissal should be handled by a complaints board. It is argued that judges should be more easily removable from office. But the existing measures have been designed to ensure the independence of the judiciary and its freedom from political involvement.

John Oatland, *British Civilisation*, London: Routledge, 2000 (pp.175-178)

◇◇ DEFINITIONS ◇◇◇

- **solicitors** lawyers engaged to advise on legal matters such as contracts, wills and sale of land and to appear in court on behalf of their clients
- **Law Society** the solicitors' trade union as well as their governing body
- **partnership** an association of two or more people set up for the purpose of carrying on business with a view to profit
- **conveyancing** the handling of property transactions
- **probate** the administering of a deceased person's estate
- **litigation** taking legal action
- **monopoly** market situation in which a single firm controls the providing of a good or service
- **licensed** having official permission to carry out some activity which is forbidden without a licence
- **building societies** private, non-profit making financial institutions that provide housing loans and mortgages to persons having deposited their savings with them
- **fees** payment for professional advice or special services
- **apprenticeship** a period of vocational training for which a young learner (apprentice) has signed a contract to be trained in a certain field or skill for a set amount of time by a specific employer
- **trainee** a person who is being trained on the job to learn a particular skill or acquire special knowledge
- **training** the process of acquiring particular skills or special knowledge on the job
- **barristers** lawyers who specialise in representing people at court
- **Bar (the)** body of lawyers who practise as barristers
- **Inns of Court** the four legal societies which have the exclusive right to train barristers and accept them as members
- **Council of Legal Education** the professional body which organizes and marks the *Bar Finals*, the final law examinations to become a barrister
- **self-employed** a person who works for himself, who owns a small business
- **brief(s)** the statement of a client's case
- **practice** the business organization of a professional person such as a lawyer, doctor or architect
- **take silk** to become a Queen's Counsel (QC) recognized by the wearing of a specially designed silk gown
- **judges** the impartial arbitrators who preside over courts
- **seniority** length of service in a profession or within an organization
- **retiring age** the age at which a person withdraws permanently from regular or active employment
- **dismissed** one's employment is permanently terminated on the initiative of the employer

◊◊ EXERCISES ◊◊◊

◊ EXERCISE 1 *Comprehension*

True / False Circle the correct answer and justify your choice

1. There has been little change over recent years in the social composition of those who enter the solicitor's profession. T / F
2. Solicitors' firms welcomed the end to the conveyancing monopoly. T / F
3. Trainee solicitors don't necessarily have to have a law degree. T / F
4. Solicitors belong to the Bar. T / F
5. You generally need to be referred to a barrister by a solicitor. T / F
6. Barristers generally share chambers. T / F
7. Both solicitors and barristers have to pass professional examinations at university. T / F
8. Most barristers prefer to enter other areas than working in a legal practice. T / F
9. All QCs become judges. T / F
10. Some critics say that senior judges should be able to be dismissed. T / F

◊ EXERCISE 2 *Vocabulary*

Select the alternative (a), (b) or (c) that most fully and correctly completes the statements below

1. Barristers are entitled to .... before any court in England and Wales.
   a) sit b) stand c) appear
2. If a lawyer joins the Bar, he must agree to .... the Bar Rules.
   a) abide by b) stand by c) rely on
3. The aspiring solicitor has to .... a university degree.
   a) pass b) complete c) make
4. Trainee solicitors must serve a two-year term of ....
   a) training b) traineeship c) apprenticeship
5. Judges have traditionally been appointed from the ranks of experienced ....
   a) solicitors b)academics c) barristers
6. Solicitors' firms have always been heavily dependent on ....
   a) building societies b) conveyancing fees c) partnerships
7. Junior judges are subject to .... for reasons of professional misconduct.
   a) lay off b) complaints c) dismissal
8. Parliament moved to end the solicitors' .... on the handling of property transactions.
   a) hold b) monopoly c) rights
9. It is not easy to assess the average .... of individual solicitors.
   a) earnings b) commissions c) returns
10. A barrister often only gets a day or two's .... of the trial.
   a) summons b) notice c) brief

◇ EXERCISE 3 *Grammar*

The **Infinitive** or the **Gerund**?

Choose between the **infinitive** (with or without **to**) and the **gerund**

1. A law student needs (to serve / serve / serving) a practical apprenticeship.
2. It is absolutely indispensable for a judge (to be / be / being) impartial.
3. By joining one of the four Inns of Court, a would-be barrister is able (to meet / meet / meeting) fully-fledged barristers.
4. (to learn / learn / learning) his chosen profession on the job is an essential part of a future solicitor's training.
5. The court's ruling did nothing but (to confuse / confuse / confusing) people.
6. Some law graduates really prefer (to become / become / becoming) public servants.
7. No senior judge can be appointed without first (to work / work / working) as a barrister.
8. His parents made him (to study / study / studying) law.
9. Solicitors still spend a lot of time (to brief / brief / briefing) barristers.
10. The aim of the Law Society is (to defend / defend / defending) its members' interests.

FROM THE NEWS

THE SCALES OF JUSTICE

Lawyer warns of police state

◇ EXERCISE

Read the article below and discuss or write answers to the following questions

1. What was the nature of Sir John's attack?
2. Explain his point about muggers.
3. What is Mr Bean saying about the scales of justice?
4. What are the police complaining about?
5. Should we blame the lawyers?

Lawyer warns of police state

Britain could slide into a "police state" if the scales of justice were "unbalanced", the leader of the 10,000 barristers in England and Wales said last week.

The chairman of the Bar Council, David Bean QC, used a lecture to criminal justice students at Portsmouth University to respond to an attack by the Metropolitan police commissioner, Sir John Stevens, on the criminal justice system and lawyers' role in it.

In a speech at Leicester University last week Sir John accused the system of treating victims and witnesses with contempt, and lawyers of regarding criminal trials as a tactital game. He claimed that muggers were released on bail eight or nine times before they faced trial for the first attack.

Mr Bean said: "We've heard some extreme claims from the police in recent days. It's time to inject some balance into the debate."

"None of us wants a police state, where the knee-jerk response to crime is to 'round up the usual suspects'. But if we did unbalance the scales of justice we would, before long, be on the slippery slope to a police state."

He added:"My members prosecute and defend in equal measure. They want a system that convicts the guilty and acquits the innocent."

Sir John said in his speech: "The fact is that all too often the criminal trial is simply an uneven game of tactics played out by lawyers in front of an uninformed jury with the disillusioned victims and a bemused defendant looking on."

"The public are more than disenchanted with criminal justice in this country – they are fed up with it."

He was expanding on the aims of the Search for Truth campaign launched at Scotland Yard in January by the Association of Chief Police Officers. Senior officers claimed that lawyers were obstructing justice and called for a raft of measures to put trials back on an even keel.

Sir John called for separate facilities for witnesses in court, and rules to prevent defence lawyers from "harassing" witnesses during cross-examination.

In his speech last week Mr Bean responded: "New laws are now coming in to protect witnesses. Courts are being adapted to prevent intimidation, though we do share the view that more needs to be done, especially in magistrates' courts."

Sir John's speech was seen in part as a response to an attack by the Home Secretary, David Blunkett, on low police detection rates. But Mr Bean said: "Blaming the lawyers is not a sensible answer to the Home Secretary's calls for reform of the working practices of the police."

Clare Dyer, *Guardian Weekly*,
14 March 2002 (p.8)

CHAPTER 22

THE STRUCTURE OF THE *US* COURT SYSTEM

◇ Key words and concepts

***US* Supreme Court**
***US* Courts of Appeal**
***US* District Courts**
State Supreme Court
Trial Courts
Local Courts
widely
struggles
civil (cases)
criminal (cases)
jurisdiction
immediate
account for
cases
tried
appeal
trial
evidence
previous

Instructions For Study

1° Turn to the **definitions** following the text *The Structure of the US Court System*. They refer to the specialist terms printed in **bold** type in the list of **Key words and concepts.** Study them closely and pinpoint them in the text.
2° Use an **English** language dictionary to check the meanings (in context) of the other words in the list.
3° Do the exercises to test your comprehension, vocabulary and grammar skills.

The Structure of the US Court System

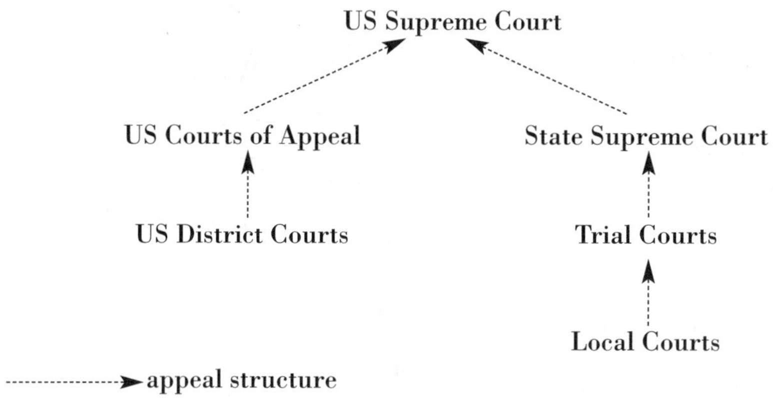

The courts play a central and influential role in American society. They directly affect the daily lives of citizens and their decisions are widely debated. Social, as well as personal, struggles are often reflected in court battles, whether civil or criminal.

American courts operate at separate *federal* and *state* levels and have their own areas of authority or jurisdiction. State courts handle the vast majority of legal work and are the most immediate for most Americans. The federal courts only account for some 2 per cent of all cases tried in the US annually.

Either party in a case may, in certain circumstances, appeal a decision to a higher court. An appeal is not a new trial, but a re-examination of the evidence, procedures and legal or constitutional principles on which the decision was based in the previous trial.

David Mauk & John Oakland, *American Civilization*,
New York: Routledge, 1995 (p.213)

◇◇ DEFINITIONS ◇◇◇

♦ ***US* Supreme Court** the final court of appeal in the *US* federal system and for some cases in the state courts
♦ ***US* Courts of Appeal** part of the federal court system, composed of 12 "circuit" courts sitting in each of 11 judicial circuits (plus the District of Columbia) and which hear appeals from decisions in the *US* district courts
♦ ***US* District Courts** part of the federal court system, composed of 92 courts situated in all parts of the *US* and handling cases involving federal litigation and breaches of federal criminal law
♦ **State Supreme Court** highest court in the state and local system which hears civil and criminal appeals from inferior state courts
♦ **Trial Courts** part of the state and local system, next up from local courts, having a more general jurisdiction and hearing civil suits and criminal cases with a jury (e.g. Family Courts, Probate Courts)
♦ **Local Courts** part of the state and local system, and hearing minor civil and criminal cases *(misdemeanours)* that often cannot be appealed and may not have a jury (e.g. Traffic Court, Small Claims Court)
♦ **civil (cases)** refer to matters involving the enforcement of a person's rights or obligations
♦ **criminal (cases)** refer to matters involving wrongs (acts harmful to the state or its citizens) for which a person can be punished
♦ **jurisdiction** the power or ability of a court to hear a case, depending on geography, area of law, type of offence or amount of remedy
♦ **cases** matters that are heard before a court
♦ **appeal** to make an appeal, i.e. when a party is not satisfied with the decision of a court, that party may ask for the case to be reheard by a higher court
♦ **trial** the stage in civil or criminal proceedings at which the evidence is examined and judgement is delivered
♦ **evidence** facts or data serving as proof of something

◇◇ EXERCISES ◇◇◇

◇ EXERCISE 1 — *Comprehension*

True / False Circle the correct choice and justify your answer

1. Many citizens question the central role played by the courts in American society. T / F
2. Most Americans have their legal affairs heard by state courts. T / F
3. By appealing a court ruling, a litigant is seeking a re-trial. T / F
4. Wider issues current in American society are often implicitly addressed by the courts. T / F
5. When re-examining evidence a higher court will summon new witnesses. T / F

◇ EXERCISE 2 *Vocabulary*

Select the verbs in the left-hand column which **match** the nouns in the right-hand one

1. to file	a) a crime
2. to enforce	b) the right
3. to deliver	c) an appeal
4. to pass	d) a judge
5. to weigh up	e) the law
6. to claim	f) a dispute
7. to hear	g) a verdict
8. to appoint	h) the evidence
9. to commit	i) a case
10. to resolve	j) sentence

◇ EXERCISE 3 *Grammar*

Spelling

Fill in the blanks with **their, there** or **they're**

1. According to FBI statistics, ... was an increase in the number of major crimes in the United States in 2001 for the first time in a decade.
2. .... are specialized federal courts in Washington, DC which settle cases in technical areas such as customs, patents and tax.
3. .... currently trying several cases involving breaches of federal criminal law.
4. The law requires that criminals be tried and punished for .... crimes, but .... is a recent Supreme Court ruling barring the execution of mentally retarded offenders.
5. .... arguing of the case was based on striking a balance between the rights of sex offenders and the safety of everyone else.
6. .... bringing a class-action lawsuit against the state of Connecticut's Internet registry of sex offenders.

THE *US* SUPREME COURT

◊ Key words and concepts

***US* Supreme Court**
Congress
lesser
three-tier system
tax
customs
patent
jurisdiction
cases
appeals
further to
hearing
arising
treaties
officials
handed down
justices
terms of office
will
chief justice
retirement
impeached
life terms
Senate
nominee
fame
judicial review
in accordance with
void
deems
granted
checks and balances
claimed
stages
extended
executive acts
upheld
encroaching
settlers
lack
carry out
rulings
enforce
urged
nullify
Union
Civil War
status

Instructions For Study

1° Turn to the **definitions** following the text *The US Supreme Court.* They refer to the specialist terms printed in **bold** type in the list of **Key words and concepts.** Study them closely and pinpoint them in the text.
2° Use an **English** language dictionary to check the meanings (in context) of the other words in the list.
3° Do the exercises to test your comprehension, vocabulary and grammar skills.

The *US* Supreme Court

The only court specifically mentioned in the Constitution is the *US Supreme Court.* However, the constitutional power given to Congress to establish lesser federal courts has resulted in a three-tier system as well as special courts for specific areas such as tax, customs, patent, and military law. *District courts* have original jurisdiction in most federal cases. Only about one-sixth of the decisions of these courts are appealed further to the next tier, the *US courts of appeals.*

Most of the US Supreme Court's work consists of hearing cases from US courts of appeals or state supreme courts. All of these cases raise federal questions (controversies arising under the Constitution, federal law or treaties). In addition it has original jurisdiction in cases which involve a state or officials of the federal government. In 1990 it heard 10 cases under its original jurisdiction and handed down decisions on 130 cases that it selected from 4,500 appeals for review. The decisions of lower courts became final in those cases it refused to hear.

The Constitution creates a separate judicial branch with a single supreme court that has an unspecified number of justices with terms of office dependent only on their 'good behaviour'. In practice, the number of justices has varied between five and ten, according to the will of Congress, but in recent history has been eight, plus a chief justice. Terms of office have by tradition been for life or until voluntary retirement. As no justice has ever been impeached, life terms have given justices an impressive degree of independence. Of the 144 men and two women nominated to the Court, about four in five have been confirmed by the Senate.

Today the fame and influence of the Supreme Court result from its power of *judicial review* (the right to evaluate whether state, congressional and presidential acts are in accordance with the Constitution and to declare them void if it deems them unconstitutional). This power, which is not explicity granted in the Constitution, gives the Court an important role in the system of checks and balances.

The Court claimed the right of judicial review by stages and won gradual acceptance for its practice between 1796 and 1865. In the first year the Court asserted its right to invalidate state laws that it considered unconstitutional. In *Marbury v. Madison* [1803], it claimed the power to invalidate an unconstitutional federal law. Later decisions extended judicial review to cover executive acts and emphasized that the Court's exercise of its review power was necessary to maintain the supremacy of federal law and a uniform interpretation of the Constitution from state to state.

President Andrew Jackson ignored the Court's decision in 1832 when it upheld the sovereignty of the Cherokee nation against encroaching settlers. Emphasizing the Court's lack of financial or military power to carry out its rulings, he remarked, '[Chief Justice] John Marshall has made his decision – now let him enforce it!' States' righters from Thomas Jefferson to those who urged Southern secession insisted that the states rather than the Court had the power to nullify federal law. As a practical fact, only the Union victory in the Civil War established the supremacy of federal law and the Constitution, and the status of the Court as their interpreter.

David Mauk & John Oakland, *American Civilization*,
New York: Routledge, 1995 (pp.153-156)

◇◇ DEFINITIONS ◇◇◇

- ♦ ***US* Supreme Court** the final court of appeal in the *US* federal system and for some cases in the state courts
- ♦ **Congress** the legislative branch of government in the USA, composed of the Senate and the House of Representatives
- ♦ **tax** matters involving the payments made to legal authorities to meet public expenses
- ♦ **customs** matters involving the control of the import and export of goods and the collection of import duties (taxes) by the government
- ♦ **patent** protection granted by the government giving someone the exclusive right to manufacture, sell or use an invention or a new industrial process
- ♦ **jurisdiction** the power of a court to hear a case
- ♦ **cases** matters that are heard before a court
- ♦ **appeals** when parties are not satisfied with the decision of a court and ask for the case to be reheard before a higher court
- ♦ **hearing** listening to and assessing evidence brought before the court
- ♦ **treaties** formal agreements between two or more states relating to peace, trade or alliance
- ♦ **justices** judges belonging to the Supreme Court
- ♦ **term of office** the length of time a person remains in an official position
- ♦ **chief justice** the presiding judge in the Supreme Court
- ♦ **retirement** permanent withdrawal from regular or active employment
- ♦ **impeached** to be charged with serious wrongdoing which may lead to removal from office
- ♦ **Senate** the upper assembly of the *US* Congress to which two senators are elected by each state
- ♦ **nominee** a person nominated by the President and whose appointment is subject to Senate approval
- ♦ **judicial review** the power of the *US* Supreme Court to make judgements on the constitutionality of acts of the national government and of the state governments
- ♦ **void** of no legal effect
- ♦ **checks and balances** a system of linking the three equal and separate branches of government (executive, legislative and judicial), enabling the national government and its separate institutions to be controlled
- ♦ **executive acts** refer to the actions of the members of the executive arm of *US* government – the President and his ministers (called secretaries) – who cannot be members of the legislature (i.e. Congress)
- ♦ **rulings** the official decisions handed down by courts
- ♦ **enforce** to compel observance of a law or ruling
- ♦ **nullify** to make legally null and void, invalidate
- ♦ **Union** the Northern states during the American Civil War (as opposed to the secessionist, Southern states)
- ♦ **Civil War** commenced when eleven slave states in America broke away to form the Southern Confederacy (1861-1865)

◇◇ EXERCISES ◇◇◇

◇ EXERCISE 1 *Comprehension*

True / False Circle the correct choice and justify your answer

1. Justices can be removed from office according to the will of Congress. T / F
2. The Supreme Court has the right of judicial review over congressional acts. T / F
3. The Supreme Court is the final court of appeal in the *US* federal system. T / F
4. The majority of the decisions handed down by district courts go on to the *US* courts of appeals. T / F
5. Most presidential nominees to the Supreme Court are confirmed by the Senate. T / F
6. The federal system is an integral part of the concept of checks and balances. T / F
7. The legislative branch of government in the USA is the House of Representatives. T / F
8. The Supreme Court does not have the right of judicial review as far as the action of the President and his ministers are concerned. T / F
9. The Civil War was instrumental in consolidating the status of the Supreme Court. T / F
10. The structure of the *US* court system is clearly outlined in the Constitution. T / F

◇ EXERCISE 2 *Vocabulary*

Select the verbs in the left-hand column which **match** the nouns in the right-hand one

1. to adjourn	a) the constitution
2. to impeach	b) a decision
3. to register	c) compensation
4. to preside over	d) a senator
5. to uphold	e) the rights
6. to review	f) an amendment
7. to overturn	g) imports
8. to share	h) a court
9. to hand down	i) an official
10. to administer	j) jurisdiction
11. to safeguard	k) a hearing
12. to claim	l) a law
13. to interpret	m) a patent
14. to elect	n) a ruling
15. to control	o) justice

◇ EXERCISE 3 *Grammar*

Conditional sentences

Complete the following sentences using the correct **tense** of the verb in brackets

1. If the witness (refuse) to testify, he will be guilty of contempt of court.
2. The judge would be more lenient, if the defendant (cooperate) with the police.
3. If you (sue) your builder, you would be paid damages.
4. You would have been able to apply for citizenship, if the Constitution (amend).
5. I would have filed an appeal, if I (know) my rights.
6. If the Supreme Court is challenged on this issue, it (set off) a constitutional crisis.
7. If the president (impeach), there will be a political crisis.
8. You would make a small fortune, if you (obtain) a patent.
9. The defendant would have gone free, if the court (uphold) the appeal.
10. You would have been vindicated, if the appeal (reach) the Supreme Court.

FROM THE NEWS

SEPARATION OF CHURCH AND STATE

Court upholds voucher plan for religious schools

◇ EXERCISE

Read the article below and discuss or write answers to the following questions

1. What did the Supreme Court rule?
2. Does its ruling contravene the First Amendment?
3. Do all the justices agree with the ruling?
4. What are the likely ramifications of the debate?
5. Have we heard the last of this?

Court upholds voucher plan for religious schools

WASHINGTON: In one of its most important rulings on education in years, the Supreme Court declared Thursday that it can be constitutional for public money to underwrite tuition at religious schools.

The justices voted, 5 to 4, to uphold Cleveland's school-voucher program and, by extension, similar programs across the country. Such programs are valid as long as parents can choose among a range of secular and religious schools, the majority said.

"In sum, the Ohio program is entirely neutral with respect to religion," Chief Justice William Rehnquist wrote for the court. "It provides benefits directly to a wide spectrum of individuals, defined only by financial need and residence in a particular school district. It permits such individuals to exercise genuine choice among options public and private, secular and religious."

Therefore, the chief justice wrote, the program does not offend a clause of the First Amendment that mandates a separation of church and state.

Writing a separate concurrence, Justice Clarence Thomas said programs like Cleveland's could be beacons of hope to impoverished inner-city children. Quoting Frederick Douglass, he wrote: "Education means emancipation. It means light and liberty. It means the uplifting of the soul of man into the glorious light of truth, the light by which men can only be made free."

But Justice John Paul Stevens called the ruling, which overturned a finding by the U.S. Court of Appeals in Cincinnati, "profoundly misguided." He wrote, "Whenever we remove a brick from the wall that was designed to separate religion and government, we increase the risk of religious strife and weaken the foundation of our democracy."

Another dissenter, Justice David Souter, said that if there were ever a good excuse to skirt the First Amendment clause, it might be found in Cleveland, whose public schools have had a woeful performance and where thousands of parents have used vouchers to send their children to private schools.

"But there is no excuse," Souter said. "Constitutional limitations are placed on government to preserve constitutional values in hard cases, like these."

Spirited public debate over voucher systems is certain to continue. Now, the arena may shift to the nation's legislative chambers.

Joining Rehnquist and Thomas in the majority were Justices Sandra Day O'Connor, Antonin Scalia and Anthony Kennedy.

Joining Stevens and Souter in dissent were Justices Ruth Bader Ginsburg and Stephen Breyer.

As the tone of the opinions indicated, the continuing debate about school-voucher programs involves issues that are not only constitutional but deeply personal as well. The debate touches not only upon separation of church and state but on how best to educate America's children.

President George W. Bush and many political conservatives support vouchers, and the ruling was a resounding victory for them. Opponents of voucher programs say they weaken already struggling public schools by draining tax money from them.

The ruling went against a 1973 ruling by a more liberal Supreme Court that struck down a New York, tuition-assistance program.

The new case was argued before the Supreme Court on Feb. 20. The importance of the case was signaled by the court's allowing 80 minutes for lawyers' presentations, a rare departure from the usual one-hour limit.

On Feb. 20, supporters of the Cleveland voucher system called it "a limited program targeted to the most needy, the poorest of the poor, who would not otherwise have a choice," in the words of Judith French, an Ohio assistant attorney general. Nearly 4,000 of Cleveland's 57,000 pupils in elementary public schools take part. The vouchers are worth up to $2,250.

As important as the ruling was, it may not be the Supreme Court's final word on the issue. On a few issues of transcendent importance, the Supreme Court has reversed its own rulings.

"I hope that a future court will reconsider today's dramatic departure," Souter wrote at the end of his dissent.

David Stout,

CHAPTER 23

LAWYERS IN AMERICA

◊ Key words and concepts

distrust
lawyers
business
attorneys at law
counsellors
drafting
contracts
trusts
wills
settle
criminal cases
civil cases
law school
status
grounding
case work
eventually
practice
cater for
corporate
sole practitioners
range
two-partner firms
trial lawyer
perform
share
associates
salary
income
on average
partnership
fees
features
contingency fee
injury
charged
rates
damages
awarded
pro-bono legal help
provided
afford
provision
overly
concerned
drive up
ABA

Instructions For Study

1° Turn to the **definitions** following the text *Lawyers in America*. They refer to the specialist terms printed in **bold** type in the list of **Key words and concepts.** Study them closely and pinpoint them in the text.
2° Use an **English** language dictionary to check the meanings (in context) of the other words in the list.
3° Do the exercises to test your comprehension, vocabulary and grammar skills.

Lawyers in America

Americans tend to distrust lawyers, although they do need their services in many cases. This antagonism might be partly due to the large number of lawyers, who appear at all levels of society. In addition to their legal roles, they are very visible in business, politics and public life. One in 440 adult Americans is a lawyer and in Washington, DC, the ratio is one in 64.

The legal profession is undivided and there are no formal distinctions between categories of lawyers. Its members, called attorneys at law, counsellors or simply lawyers, exercise broad functions, although some may specialize in one branch of the law. They give general legal assistance such as the drafting of contracts, trusts, or wills; settle conflicts outside court; and also present criminal or civil cases in court.

Most lawyers today will have first obtained a law degree from the law school of a university. The value of the law degree varies greatly with the status of the law school, although the best are world-famous. The degree gives the lawyer a general grounding in American law through academic lectures and practical case work. But lawyers also have to know the law of the state in which they will eventually practise and must pass the appropriate state bar examination. Lawyers may work for federal and state government or in industry and commerce. But the large majority are in private practice and cater for individual and corporate clients. Some work by themselves as sole practitioners in small communities and serve a wide range of clients. But most lawyers practise in firms. Half of them work in two-partner firms consisting of an office attorney and a trial lawyer, who perform different functions. The other half work in bigger firms, which have a variable number of lawyers and may have offices worldwide. The three categories of lawyers in big firms are senior partners and junior partners who receive a share of the profits and associates who are paid a fixed salary.

The lawyer's income is frequently a high one, at least in the medium-to-big firms and is, on average, one of the highest in the country. The top students of the best law schools are normally able to join an important law firm at a good salary and may quickly proceed to a partnership.

The financing of a law firm, in addition to ordinary commercial fees, may include other features. The contingency fee (payment upon results in personal injury cases) can be charged at rates which may reach 50 per cent of the damages awarded. But *pro-bono* legal help without fees may be provided for those who cannot afford to pay for legal services and firms may participate in state and federal legal aid programmes for the poor. The provision of government legal aid is an important and expensive federal programme, particularly since fees for legal services are generally very high. The public also seem to think that lawyers are overly concerned with money and that they drive up costs and their fees.

Lawyers have organized themselves at national and state levels into bar associations (or lawyers' organizations), which supervise the profession, protect professional interests and discipline their members. The American Bar Association (ABA) was created nationally in 1878. But only about one-half of all lawyers are ABA members. Most states require that lawyers must be members of the state bar association, which is affiliated to the ABA. But in other states a lawyer may practise law without being a member of the state bar association.

David Mauk & John Oakland, *American Civilization*,
New York: Routledge, 1995 (pp.221-223)

◊◊ DEFINITIONS ◊◊◊

♦ **lawyers** people who have studied law and who are legally authorized to represent people in court or in other circumstances
♦ **business** the business world, i.e. all areas of trading and commercial activity
♦ **attorneys at law / counsellors** synonyms for lawyers in the USA
♦ **contract** a legally binding agreement between two or more parties
♦ **trust** the legal document stating that property is being held and administered by someone (a *trustee*) for the benefit of some other person (the *beneficiary*)
♦ **will** the written expression of a person's desires concerning what is to happen to his property and belongings after his death
♦ **criminal cases** matters involving wrongs (acts harmful to the state or its citizens) for which a person can be punished
♦ **civil cases** matters involving the enforcement of a person's rights or obligations
♦ **case work** a method of learning law in which the student works out solutions to actual or hypothetical law problems
♦ **practice** the business organization of a professional person such as lawyer, doctor or architect
♦ **corporate** relating to a business organization (corporation) or enterprise
♦ **sole practitioners** people who own and operate a business enterprise by themselves
♦ **trial lawyer** the attorney who represents his clients in court
♦ **associates** the salaried lawyers of a law firm
♦ **salary** the fixed compensation paid monthly to the employee of an organization which does not depend directly on the number of hours worked
♦ **income** earnings
♦ **partnership** an association of two or more people set up for the purpose of carrying on business with a view to profit
♦ **fees** payment for professional advice or special services
♦ **contingency fee** the system whereby a lawyer's remuneration in the USA is tied to the success of the action undertaken, e.g. a percentage of the damages awarded
♦ **rates** the amount of fees charged expressed as a percentage
♦ **damages** compensation in the form of money that the court orders one party to pay another
♦ **pro-bono legal help** is legal work undertaken free of charge in the USA for people on low incomes
♦ **ABA (American Bar Association)** an influential, private voluntary association to which about one-half of the attorneys in the USA belong and which gives accreditation to law schools

◊◊ EXERCISES ◊◊◊

◊ EXERCISE 1 *Comprehension*

Answer these questions

1. Why are some Americans distrustful of lawyers?
2. What is meant by "the legal profession is undivided"?
3. Does a lawyer's legal education end at university?
4. Do law firms earn all their income from the ordinary fees paid for their services?
5. Do lawyers belong to a professional association of some kind?

◊ EXERCISE 2 *Vocabulary*

Select the alternative (a), (b) or (c) that most fully and correctly completes the statements below

1. The figures show that the US has a high crime .... in comparison with Britain.
   a) number b) percentage c) rate
2. The ABA is very .... in the nomination of judges.
   a) influencing b) influential c) influenced
3. The case method is based on a very .... approach to teaching law.
   a) academic b) practical c) philosophical
4. Legal aid can be provided .... to people with low earnings.
   a) free of charge b) gratuitously c) graciously
5. He always takes a fixed percentage of compensation ....
   a) levied b) sought c) granted
6. The parties to a contractual agreement are legally .... by it.
   a) held b) bound c) tied up
7. This legal firm is .... by a single person.
   a) run b) driven c) directed
8. Attorneys at law assist in the .... of various legal documents.
   a) composition b)settling c) drawing up

◊ EXERCISE 3 *Grammar*

Phrasal Verbs

Complete the following sentences with a suitable **particle** from the list below

out / for / down / out of / over / up / forward

1. A number of convincing arguments were put .... by counsel for the defence.
2. The case for the prosecution ran .... steam.
3. The litigant had taken action to sue .... damages.
4. The court issued a declaration setting .... the plaintiff's legal rights.
5. The Supreme Court is presided .... by the Chief Justice.
6. The court allowed .... mitigating circumstances.
7. Lawyers give assistance in the drawing .... of contracts.
8. The higher court overturned the ruling handed .... by the local court.

EDITORIAL OPINION

MASS TORTS

No way to right a wrong

◇ EXERCISE

(A) Read the editorial below and discuss or write answers to the following questions

1. What is the **subject** of this editorial?
2. Quote the sentence that best expresses **editorial opinion.**
3. Is the **title** an appropriate one?
4. Describe the **tone** adopted by the editorialist.
5. Do you think litigation can get out of hand?

(B) Select the alternative (a), (b) or (c) which corresponds to the **editorial opinion** expressed

1. Lawyers are taking .... advantage of business opportunities afforded by mass torts.
   a) increasing b) decreasing c) little
2. Claimants receive .... compensation for damages incurred.
   a) sufficient b) little c) insufficient
3. Politicians .... the recycling of settlement money.
   a) benefit from b) hesitate over c) will reform
4. Companies should .... be held accountable for corporate carelessness.
   a) not b) fully c) partly
5. Companies should be forced to foot the bill in .... circumstances.
   a) all b) some c) no
6. A registry of potential claimants would be a (n) .... solution.
   a) adequate b) inadequate c) part
7. Claims should be judged ....
   a) on a block basis b) on their own merits c) in tort havens
8. Solutions resulting in less money for lawyers are a (n) ....
   a) fantasy b) drawback c) advantage

No way to right a wrong

Cancerous product, cancerous litigation

What should America do about mass torts? The toll from asbestos litigation continues to mount. ABB, a European engineering firm, is the latest company to face ruin because of work done by a subsidiary that was not only legal at the time, but carried out in the interest of safety. And asbestos is only one cause of such litigation. Tobacco, lead paint and pharmaceutical products are all ripe business opportunities for lawyers, who routinely earn 30-50% of settlements.

A paper published earlier this year by the Council of Economic Advisers estimates that America's tort system soaks up 1.8% of GPD, or $180 billion a year. And for little purpose: only 20% of the money goes to claimants for economic damages. In a number of mass tort cases, courts have begged Congress to intervene. But politicians hesitate. Reform would reduce payments to a constituency that recycles settlement money into political contributions: the trial lawyers.

Certainly, companies must take responsibility for disclosing the known potential hazards of the products they produce, and for shouldering the consequences when they do not. But asbestos does harm in a particularly insidious way. Its horrible cancers and respiratory problems may emerge only long after the statute of limitations has expired, meaning that there may be no redress even for medical costs. This lag has encouraged lawyers to seek huge settlements for people who are not harmed and will never be harmed. The result is not only to wreak havoc upon companies forced to pay the bill, but in effect to limit the compensation for real victims.

Two remedies that are being widely discussed for asbestos could be used elsewhere. The more modest is to create a registry of people who might eventually be able to file a tort claim for exposure to a toxic substance, to preserve their right to litigate beyond any normal statute of limitation. Courts in Pennsylvania and Massachusetts have already begun to do this. But it can only be a partial solution. No one would want to be at the end of the line in cases with huge potential financial settlements, because there may be nothing left when their turn comes. The registry also leaves a huge liability hanging over existing businesses.

A second idea is to address mass torts by creating a giant administrative compensation system, along the lines of the fund for victims of the September 11th attacks. The fund could compensate for economic damage – lost wages and medical costs – rather than for the more abstract "pain and suffering" that largely feeds the plaintiff bar. But cutting out the plaintiff bar would undoubtedly jeopardise passage through Congress.

Think modest

The best approach would be twofold. First, as suggested by Victor Schwartz of the Campaign for Asbestos Justice, limit litigation to where plaintiffs live, or were exposed, or where the defendant has its principal place or business. That would control the rush to tort havens in Mississippi, West Virginia, Texas and Illinois, where verdicts are most irresponsibly open-handed. Defendants complain that, in a handful of jurisdictions, judges allow the introduction of poor scientific evidence and block depositions by plaintiffs, with devastating consequences. Second, end the consolidation of claims that have little to do with one another. In a recent case in West Virginia, more than 8,000 plaintiffs took 250 companies to court. After pre-trial settlements, there were still 5,000 plaintiffs when the trial began. Supreme Court rulings may also help.

Solutions exist. But all have one dire weakness: less money for lawyers. Could Congress ever swallow that – even to benefit true victims of corporate carelessness?

The Economist, 26 October 2002 (p.16)

GLOSSARY EXERCISES

PART A : ECONOMIC HISTORY

Circle the alternative (a), (b) or (c) which **matches** the definition

1. People who pay rent to landlords for the use of land or property
   (a) yeomen (b) producers (c) tenants
2. Sector in which the work is done in the producer's own home
   (a) manufacturing industry (b) cottage industry (c) primary industry
3. Total revenue from sales before any expenditure on raw materials or equipment
   (a) net income (b) gross income (c) sales revenue
4. Skilled workmen or artisans who use their hands to make things
   (a) craftsmen (b) labourers (c) manufacturers
5. Financial assistance to the needy
   (a) relief (b) wages (c) poor rate
6. Goods produced using inputs
   (a) supply (b) output (c) production
7. A primary product such as corn, wool or tea
   (a) manufacture (b) convenience good (c) commodity
8. Payments made to the legal authorities to meet public expenses
   (a) levies (b) contributions (c) taxes
9. An association of tradesmen or artisans which controlled production of a particular commodity or service and regulated the admission of members
   (a) trade union (b) guild (c) sect
10. Adults in employment or looking for a job
    (a) labor force (b) staff (c) personnel
11. The income accruing to the entrepreneur
    (a) salary (b) profit (c) receipts

12. The owner of land who rents it to others
    (a) rentier (b) peasant (c) landlord
13.A reserve of money put aside for a specific purpose
    (a) deposit (b) fund (c) asset
14.The worker's ablity or capacity to produce
    (a) labor power (b) work force (c) surplus value
15. A sum paid to the landlord for the use of land
    (a) rates (b) rent (c) tax
16. A manual occupation requiring a high degree of skill
    (a) trade (b) job (c) entrepreneur
17. Buyers of products and services who use them to satisfy their needs
    (a) suppliers (b) traders (c) consumers
18. A plant cultivated in large quantities on farms and in fields (e.g. wheat)
    (a) harvest (b) crop (c) seed
19. Something used in manufacturing and transformed to make a finished product
    (a) primary produce (b) foodstuffs (c) raw materials
20. Shipping of goods from one country to another for sale or exchange
    (a) import (b) export (c) haulage

PART B : ECONOMIC THOUGHT

Select the concept (a), (b) or (c) which **matches** the definition

1. The quantity of a good available on the market
   (a) offer (b) provision (c) supply
2. The return on the use of land, labor or capital
   (a) income (b) revenue (c) proceeds
3. The amount of goods and services you can actually buy with your money income
   (a) consumer power (b) buying ability (c) purchasing power
4. The maximum level of output attainable by using present machinery to capacity
   (a) spare capacity (b) full capacity (c) idle capacity
5. Accumulating deliberately beyond normal needs
   (a) hoarding (b) saving (c) sparing
6. Income for manual labor
   (a) salary (b) wages (c) cash
7. A slowdown in economic activity
   (a) depression (b) crash (c) recession
8. An insufficient supply of something
   (a) shortage (b) thrift (c) surplus
9. An increase in a nation's output of goods and services over time
   (a) growth (b) stock (c) recovery

10. Government department which controls the import and export of goods and collects duties
    (a) quarantine (b) customs (c) Internal Revenue Service
11. Organization of workers set up to protect and promote their rights and interests
    (a) labour exchange (b) claimants' union (c) trade union
12. All the characteristics of a product which enable people to derive utility from it
    (a) surplus value (b) exchange value (c) use value
13. Postponing current consumption to accumulate wealth
    (a) saving (b) spending (c) stockpiling
14. The quantity of items produced per worker per unit of time
    (a) labor intensiveness (b) labor productivity (c) production
15. Rivalry between different firms for the same customers
    (a) competetiveness (b) concurrence (c) competition
16. The ability to use one's knowledge or proficiency to perform a task
    (a) specialization (b) skill (c) know-how
17. An agent who buys and sells stocks and shares on a stock exchange
    (a) shareholder (b) stockman (c) stockbroker
18. The worker's ability or capacity to produce
    (a) labor power (b) work force (c) surplus value
19. A large and persistent fall in the level of output and employment
    (a) slump (b) crisis (c) depression
20. Customs duties levied by a government on imported or exported goods
    (a) rates (b) tariffs (c) sales tax

PART C : POLITICAL ECONOMY

Select the definition in the right-hand column which **matches** the concept in the left-hand one

1. legal tender	(a) the profit remaining after deducting all selling expenses and operating costs from the gross profit of an enterprise
2. advertising	(b) the actual rate of monetary return on an investment
3. interest	(c) shareholders have no legal obligation to settle any debts incurred by a company beyond the extent of their investment (shareholding) in it
4. GDP	(d) the bank notes and coins in circulation in an economy used as a medium of exchange
5. hire	(e) income for labor
6. return	(f) a diagram, graph or table, drawn to present facts and figures (data)
7. markets	(g) expenditure on assets (property) aimed at returning an income

8. imports	(h) a price index that shows the ratio of a nation's export prices to its import prices
9. instalment	(i) amounts of stock placed in circulation by a company at a particular time
10. public spending	(j) payments made to the legal authorities to meet public expenses
11. issues	(k) amounts of money owed by one party to another
12. net profit	(l) the average age to which a category of persons will live
13. sale	(m) expenditure by central (or federal) government and state or local authorities on goods and services
14. investments	(n) the field of study involving the task of collecting, classifying and analysing figures related to observable fact
15. statistics	(o) the business of making a product or service known to consumers
16. competitors	(p) to take a worker on, to pay someone to do a job
17. currency	(q) goods and services bought from other countries
18. debts	(r) firms which are rivals in business; business rivals
19. chart	(s) a partial payment of a debt
20. terms-of-trade	(t) the market value of the total output of a country's economy
21. taxes	(u) the selling of something for money
22. exchange rate	(v) the place where goods and services are sold
23. limited liability	(w) money which, by law, must be accepted in payment of a debt or obligation
24. wages	(x) the price of one currency in terms of another
25. life expectancy	(y) a sum of money paid for the use of capital, usually expressed as a rate or percentage

PART D : LABOR ECONOMICS

Exercise 1
Fill in the blanks with the words from the list below

union / born / active / managerial / members / arrangements / dues / official / apprenticeship / retirement / benefits / white-collar / shop / trade / conditions / job / support / baby-boom / union / employment / workers / rate

1. Working .... are factors affecting the work environment, such as hours of work, safety ...., fringe ....
2. A plant or establishment in which only union .... can be hired is called a closed ....
3. .... is permanent withdrawal from regular or .... employment.
4. Adults in................or looking for a .... constitute the labor force.
5. ....strikes are those that take place in accordance with .... instructions.
6. .... cohorts are groups of individuals .... between 1946 and 1962 when

there was a marked increase in the birth ....

7. A .... union in no longer allowed to call out its workers in .... of industrial action by unionists elsewhere.
8. .... are the contributions that a .... member pays regularly to his organization.
9. Skilled .... are those who have acquired, through training or ...., the special abilities required to do certain work.
10. .... workers are office workers, clerical staff, ... and professional people.

Exercise 2

Circle the alternative (a), (b) or (c) which **matches** the definition

1. Moving from one's country of residence or birth to settle in another
   (a) settlement (b) exile (c) migration
2. Compensation or remuneration paid to individuals in an organization
   (a) earnings (b) profits (c) returns
3. Facts or data serving as proof of something
   (a) evidence (b) estimations (c) hypotheses
4. The upper stratum of the working class
   (a) the proletariate (b) the labour aristocracy (c) blue collars
5. The selling functions of a business enterprise
   (a) trading (b) sales (c) marketing
6. The situation of being jobless when willing and able to work
   (a) idleness (b) redundancy (c) unemployment
7. Persons holding responsibility in business organisations for making decisions
   (a) executives (b) operatives (c) organizers
8. Adults in employment or looking for a job
   (a) the labour stock (b) the labour count (c) the labour force
9. A large and persistent fall in the level of output and employment
   (a) depression (b) recession (c) stagflation
10. The work force or personnel of an organization
    (a) the working population (b) staff (c) white collars

PART E : MANAGEMENT

Exercise 1

Select the verbs in the left-hand column which **match** the nouns in the right-hand one

1. to earn	a) a policy
2. to make	b) a meeting
3. to cash	c) money
4. to implement	d) growth
5. to call	e) demand
6. to lower	f) imports
7. to cut	g) (interest) rates
8. to devalue	h) a cheque
9. to boost	i) a currency
10. to meet	j) an investment

Exercise 2
Complete the following sentences with the suitable **particle** from the list below

down / back / out / ahead / off / up / in

1. Investors are working .... the new value of the stocks.
2. If they want to succeed, they will have to push .... aggressively.
3. A few companies have piled .... debts in recent years.
4. Investors are cutting .... on trading
5. They prefer to stand .... than to take a risk.
6. The manager advised his staff to look .... for opportunities.
7. It now seems clear that neither side is likely to back ....
8. That country is hoping to pull .... of recession.
9. The bank decided to cut .... the company's financial lifeline.
10. Money-losing companies will be shut ....

Exercise 3
Circle the alternative (a), (b) or (c) which **matches** the definition

1. Buying items from home by means of computers and cable or satellite television
   (a) teleshopping b) electronic home shopping (c) telemarketing
2. People recommended to your company as possible customers
   (a) referrals (b) lapsed customers (c) prospects
3. Mail which is sent to a prospect who is not a suitable target
   (a) mail order (b) direct mail (c) junk mail
4. Marketing communications system whereby trained specialists use telecommunications and information technologies to conduct marketing and sales activities
   (a) inbound telemarketing (b) telemarketing (c) outbound telemarketing
5. Long-term decisions and plans made by directors setting the course an organisation must follow
   (a) tactical decisions (b) operational decisions (c) strategic decisions
6. The influence the wider economic situation, the customers, the suppliers and the competitors have on the performance of an organisation
   (a) marketing mix (b) marketing plan (c) business environment
7. One of the stages during which shares can be issued for payment over a period of time
   (a) call (b) rights issue (c) bonus issue
8. Legal responsibility for company debts
   (a) limited liability (b) unlimited liability (c) liability
9. Another term for a share-buying institution is
   (a) underwriter (b) merchant bank (c) institutional investor
10. Financial offer made by a firm wanting to buy another in order to absorb it
   (a) acquisition (b) takeover (c) takeover bid
11. Official registration of a company with the stock exchange enabling it to sell shares directly to the public

(a) listing (b) shareholding (c) trading

12. Reduction in the unit cost of products achieved as a result of an increase in the size of the organisation, in the output or as a result of better technology, management and business practices
    (a) economy of scale (b) economics of scale (c) economies of scale
13. Firms facilitating the distribution of products to customers
    (a) channel intermediaries (b) wholesalers (c) retailers
14. A company, usually an MNE , which owns and controls other smaller companies
    (a) holding (b) subsidiary (c) parent company
15. Process by which an organisation offers unique products to satisfy the particular needs of customers
    (a) centralisation (b) customisation (c) decentralisation

PART F : LAW

Select the definition which **matches** the concept in the left-hand column

Exercise 1

1. contract	(a) the statement of a client's case
2. appeal	(b) compensation in the form of money that the court orders one party to pay another
3. plaintiff	(c) a punishment ordered by a court in which the guilty party must pay a specific sum of money
4. case work	(d) a lawyer engaged to advise on legal matters such as contracts, wills and sale of land and to appear in court on behalf of his clients
5. justices	(e) matters that are heard before a court
6. brief	(f) the legal document stating that property is being held and administered by someone (a trustee) for the benefit of some other person (the beneficiary)
7. damages	(g) the legal solution to a matter brought before the court by a plaintiff
8. wrong	(h) the person who has committed a crime
9. fine	(i) a method of learning law in which the student works out solutions to actual or hypothetical law problems
10. trust	(j) when a party is not satisfied with the decision of a court, that party may ask for the case to be reheard by a higher court
11. hearing	(k) a legally binding agreement between two or more parties
12. solicitor	(l) an act that causes injury to others and for which compensation (damages) can be claimed in civil proceedings
13. statute law	(m) the party bringing an action in a civil case
14. judicial review	(n) of no legal effect

15. bill	(o) when the defendant is declared guilty at the conclusion of a trial
16. offender	(p) the name given to proposed legislation when it is introduced and debated in Parliament
17. case	(q) power of the *US* Supreme Court to make judgements on the constitutionality of acts of the national government and of the state governments
18. remedy	(r) listening to and assessing evidence brought before the court
19. conviction	(s) the judges belonging to the Supreme Court
20. void	(t) all law made by parliament

Exercise 2

1. sue	(a) official decisions made by judges
2. jurisdiction	(b) the four legal societies which have the exclusive right to train barristers and accept them as members
3. precedent	(c) the attorney who represents his clients in court
4. will	(d) the legislative branch of government in the USA, composed of the Senate and the House of Representatives
5. prosecute	(e) matters dealing with wrongs (acts harmful to the state or its citizens) for which a person can be punished
6. Congress	(f) the law that does not deal with criminal matters but with enforcing rights and obligations
7. trial	(g) payment for professional advice or special services
8. partnership	(h) to bring criminal proceedings against an accused person
9. common law	(i) the notion that people will be treated fairly by the state and that no-one is above the law
10. defendant	(j) to bring a civil action against someone
11. impeach	(k) the stage in civil or criminal proceedings at which the evidence is examined and judgement is delivered
12. civil law	(l) the written expression of a person's desires concerning what is to happen to his property and belongings after his death
13. criminal cases	(m) an earlier judicial decision on which a judge bases later rulings
14. trial lawyer	(n) the power of a court to hear a case
15. rulings	(o) payment for loss, injury or damages
16. trespass	(p) in a legal action, the person sued or the person accused of a wrong
17. rule of law	(q) to charge a government official with serious wrongdoing which may lead to his removal from office
18. compensation	(r) an association of two or more people set up for the purpose of carrying on business with a view to profit
19. fees	(s) to enter someone's property without their permission
20. Inns of Court	(t) the law made by judges as they rule upon cases brought before them in court

INDEX OF KEY WORDS AND CONCEPTS

*References are to chapter numbers. The letter **b** after a chapter number refers to the second list of definitions in chapters where there are two lists (chapters 2, 4, 5, 16, 17, 18, 19, 20, and 22)*

Composition et mise en page : Laser Graphie – 42160 Andrézieux-Bouthéon
Impression et façonnage : France Quercy – 46090 Mercuès
Dépôt légal : septembre 2003
N° Impression : 82335 - N° éditeur : 1687
Date de réimpression : novembre 2008